praise for ignite YOUR spirit

"*Ignite Your Spirit* is positive and divinely inspired. Easy to read, it is a daily capsule for each day's digestion. The passages speak to the heart, allowing the reader to identify and grow spiritually. *Ignite Your Spirit* will help give wisdom and guidance each day."

Mary Alice, retired teacher, Indiana

"The chronological progression of texts enables the reader to know the Bible is for all time and speaks to persons in different ways. *Ignite Your Spirit* provides daily devotions concise enough to give one food for thought even on busy, hurried days."

Tom, retired business executive, and Carol, retired guidance counselor, California

"In *Ignite Your Spirit* I find having the four translations in front of the reader is very helpful in studying the entire verse…The comments are applicable to current trends and timely for the day we live in."

Cheryl, mother of four and music therapy teacher, Indiana

"*Ignite Your Spirit* with four translations makes the Bible more understandable. I like the simplicity in that one topic or feeling is expressed on each page, because it is not overwhelming for the younger reader. I think they would get this."

Gerry, Sunday school teacher, and retired nurse, Indiana

"I find the author of *Ignite Your Spirit* to be sincere, articulate, concise, and stimulating in her comments about God. Including four versions of each Scripture passage is very helpful."

Martha, mother of six, Indiana

"I think you are right on track. *Ignite Your Spirit* is very easy for everyone to understand."

Joyce, mother of four and grandmother of three, child care specialist, Indiana

"By bringing together scriptures from prominent Bible translations, linking them to current day references, *Ignite Your Spirit* reveals meaning and facilitates understanding for vital biblical scriptures."

Jeff, robotics staff engineer, Michigan

"I can't think of any better way to spend our time than in searching out the Lord to know Him better. I think *Ignite Your Spirit* will be helpful to me and understandable by young people as well. I particularly liked the *Good News Bible* version."

Jamie, mother of four, physical therapist, Indiana

"I think *Ignite Your Spirit* is a much needed tool for teens to help them learn about the Bible."

Carolyn, mother of two, two grandchildren, entrepreneur, Florida

"Having read the excerpts from *Ignite Your Spirit*, I am now looking forward to reading the entire book. It is a blessing to those who read it."

Charlie, engineer, and father of six, Indiana

"Thank you for letting me read a part of *Ignite Your Spirit*. I liked it. I think it will help change lives. And I think that you did a great job."

Kael, fourth grade, Indiana

"I read the devotionals from *Ignite Your Spirit*. I think they are great. I have a hard time reading my Bible sometimes, and reading a devotional a day is like reading my Bible. The devotions are short, but I like short. Every day I can read and meditate on one verse which really helps me understand it and come closer to God."

Rachel, sixth grade, Indiana

"Your devotionals are very original. I liked them, and I would read *Ignite Your Spirit* when it is published."

Abby, seventh grade, Indiana

"The devotionals are brief in *Ignite Your Spirit* allowing the reader to meditate on a small portion of scripture, making it more easily applicable. The translation choices offer additional insight into the passages that may have otherwise been missed in reading only one version."

Kayla, age 12, and Maelynn, age 15, home-schooled students, Indiana

"I am thankful that the Lord inspired you to write *Ignite Your Spirit*, and I believe that lots of folks will find that it does just that when they read it."

Kevin, engineer, Indiana

Ignite
YOUR
spirit

shari sousley

Ignite YOUR spirit

choose your destiny by discovering
love, joy, hope, and peace

Tate Publishing & *Enterprises*

Ignite Your Spirit
Copyright © 2008 by Shari Sousley. All rights reserved.

This title is also available as a Tate Out Loud product. Visit www.tatepublishing.com for more information.

No part of this publication may be reproduced, stored in a retrieval system or transmitted in any way by any means, electronic, mechanical, photocopy, recording or otherwise without the prior permission of the author except as provided by USA copyright law.

Scripture quotations marked "KJV" are taken from the *King James Version* (Cambridge University Press London, New York and Australia). Copyright 1972 by Thomas Nelson Inc. Camden, New Jersey 08013.

Scripture quotations marked "NISV" are taken from the *New International Study Bible*. Copyright 1995 (Zondervan Publishing House, Grand Rapids, MI).

Scripture quotations marked "GNB" are taken from the *Good News Bible Today's English Version*. Copyright 1976 (American Bible Society, New York).

Scripture quotations marked "TMB" are taken from the *NIV/The Message Parallel Bible* Zondervan Corporation Copyright 2004.

Some of scripture quotations have headings with parenthesis around them. These headings are from the *The Good News Bible Today's English Version* ("GNB") (American Bible Society, New York) copyright 1976.

The opinions expressed by the author are not necessarily those of Tate Publishing, LLC.

Published by Tate Publishing & Enterprises, LLC
127 E. Trade Center Terrace | Mustang, Oklahoma 73064 USA
1.888.361.9473 | www.tatepublishing.com

Tate Publishing is committed to excellence in the publishing industry. The company reflects the philosophy established by the founders, based on Psalm 68:11,
"The Lord gave the word and great was the company of those who published it."

Book design copyright © 2008 by Tate Publishing, LLC. All rights reserved.
Cover design by Kellie Southerland
Interior design by Stephanie Woloszyn

Published in the United States of America

ISBN: 978-1-60604-919-8
1. Inspiration: Motivational: Devotional
2. Christian Living: Spiritual Growth: Spiritual Formation
08.07.25

This book is dedicated to
the love of my life
my husband, Jim
and
Kimberly, Kael, Tom, and Carol

acknowledgments

Do you believe in miracles? The Lord has a plan for your life. He will prepare you for what lies ahead. The Lord's Spirit leads us when we give Him full control.

I hope the words of this book, through meditation and journaling will *Ignite Your Spirit* to come closer to the Lord. There are some special verses to think about each day. "The Lord knows everything we need. So don't worry about tomorrow; it will have enough worries of its own." God says, "I alone know the plans I have for you, plans to bring you prosperity and not disaster, plans to bring about the future you hope for," when "…you seek me with all your heart." "The peace that Christ gives is to guide you in the decisions you make." *So let go of the worry and give it to God.* (Paraphrased from Matthew 6:32-34, Jeremiah 29:11-12, and Colossians 3:15, GNB)

In 1998 I was led by the Lord to read the Bible through. At that time, I was not feeling well and had many sleepless nights that left me with a lot of idle time. While reading, I started comparing several translations of the Bible to clarify scriptures. I wrote the scriptures down and my thoughts for future study.

In 2005 at a Sunday morning communion service, I was prayed for and anointed. I was grateful the Lord released me from severe leg, hip, and back pain.

In 2006 my daughter was diagnosed with cancer. After many prayerful and tension-filled months, she had surgery and treatment. She is a testimony to God's grace as a cancer survivor today. We do believe in miracles.

Looking back, I can see how the Lord led me to get organized to write a book. At one of the most difficult times of my life, through prayer and studying His word, the Lord kept me focused on trusting Him. I was empowered by trusting and believing in God's power and grace. As I was praying and thanking the Lord, the Holy Spirit led me to use the comparison scriptures and journaling to write this book.

The book is easy to understand for those that do not know much about the Bible. People who know the Bible will enjoy reading the different translations of the verses. There are extra lines for journaling at the end of the book.

Trust in the Lord; He will not let you down.

Thank you to Pastor Donna at Good Shepherd United Methodist Church, for anointing and praying with me when the Lord blessed me and started my healing.

I want to thank my husband, Jim, for his ideas, countless hours of editing rewriting, and helping name the book. I also want to thank him for using his computer knowledge and assistance in putting the book together.

Thank you to Tom and Carol for their overall encouragement.

Thank you, Dennis, for giving me website ideas to research music sources.

Thank you to Kael for his encouragement and Kimberly for her ideas, editing and other input for the cover of the book. Also thanks to Kevin, Jeff, Kendra, and Davie for ideas and overall support.

Thank you to my past mentors, Gloria, Art, Paul, Mary, Jay, Janie, Ginny, Betsy, Jeanette, and Linda.

Special thanks to the people at Tate Publishing. Thank you to Ryan Tate for the opportunity to publish my book Special thanks to Stacy, Lauren my editor for her patience, Kellie my graphic designer, Stephanie in layout design, and many others for all their help in publishing *Ignite Your Spirit*.

introduction

Do you need a friend? Where do you turn when there are problems? Where do you find love, joy, hope, and peace? Where do you find nourishment for your spirit? When you are having a bad day, do you have a way to calm your fears and have inner peace? Ignite your spirit; take about 180 seconds out of your day to help you get in touch with the things in your life to help make life worth living. Pray each day before reading. Ask God to help you understand the scriptures. Only God through Jesus Christ, and the Holy Spirit, can help you find true peace in your soul.

Four different Bible translations are presented. They are the King James Bible, New International Study Bible, Good News Bible, and The Message Bible.

In each version of the Bible, the words of the scriptures are written in progressively more modern language making the meaning of the verses easier to understand. Often an entire chapter of the Bible will be printed once it has been discussed. This gives an overview of the chapter so you may get the feel of the entire passage. There are questions with some of the verses. Space is provided for writing answers or comments for your journal at the end of the book. I hope you will use the space to express your thoughts and feelings. I know you will feel the touch of the Lord Jesus Christ in your life as you study His word in a different way.

Each verse in the meditation has initials showing the Bible translation:

- King James Bible version (KJV)
- New International Study Bible version (NISV)
- Good News Bible (GNB)
- The NIV/Message Bible version (TMB)

Words in *italics* within scripture quotations have been added by the author.

january 1

Psalm 23:1
"The Lord our Shepherd"

(The entire chapter of 23rd Psalm is on January 6)

KJV: The Lord is my shepherd; I shall not want.

NISV: The Lord is my shepherd; I shall not be in want.

GNB: The Lord is my shepherd: I have everything I need.

TMB: God, my shepherd! I don't need a thing.

When people are upset, psychologists suggest that they picture a favorite peaceful setting. I find that reading and thinking about the 23rd Psalm will quiet my heart and soul. All the things that God is are contained in this beautiful psalm. The verses bring me back to everyday reality of what my life should be about. The Lord will supply all our needs. All we need to do is ask Jesus to be the Lord of our lives.

Ignite your spirit by inviting the Lord to be your shepherd. Challenge yourself to choose your destiny by focusing on discovering God's love and peace.

january 2

Psalm 23:2
"The Lord is our Shepherd"

KJV: He maketh me to lie down in green pastures: he leadeth me beside the still waters.

NISV: He makes me lie down in green pastures, he leads me beside quiet waters,

GNB: He lets me rest in fields of green grass and leads me to quiet pools of fresh water.

TMB: You have bedded me down in lush meadows, you find me quiet pools to drink from.

When I picture green pastures and quiet pools of water, I am blessed and refreshed. I think of the miracles the Lord performed for me.

Read about the miracles the Lord did in the Old and New Testament.

Do you believe in miracles?

january 3

Psalm 23:3
"The Lord is our Shepherd"

KJV: He restoreth my soul: he leadeth me in the paths of righteousness for his name's sake.

NISV: He restores my soul. He guides me in paths of righteousness for his name's sake.

GNB: He gives me new strength. He guides me in the right paths, as he has promised.

TMB: True to your word, you let me catch my breath and send me in the right direction.

When I let God restore my soul, I can feel God is with me and will lead me in the right direction. Choosing your destiny with God will give you strength.

A web site that is available for finding Bible background, scriptures, and books is: http://bible.christianity.com, *click on "A Book of Great Price: The Most Valuable Book You Own" (by David Jeremiah).*

january 4

Psalm 23:4
"The Lord is our Shepherd"

KJV: Yea, though I walk through the valley of the shadow of death, I will fear no evil: for thou art with me; thy rod and thy staff they comfort me.

NISV: Even though I walk through the valley of the shadow of death, I will fear no evil, for you are with me: your rod and your staff, they comfort me.

GNB: Even if I go through the deepest darkness, I will not be afraid, LORD, for you are with me. Your shepherd's rod and staff protect me.

TMB: Even when the way goes through Death Valley. I'm not afraid when you walk at my side. Your trusty shepherd's crook makes me feel secure.

I haven't walked through the actual shadow of death yet, but many trials and problems in my life made it seem like I was having a horrible or deathlike experience. The Lord gives us confidence that He is with us. The Bible, prayer, and Christian fellowship become our rod and staff. He is with us and will lead us if we trust Him.

Write about an experience where you felt like you needed help. Did you ask for God's help?

january 5

Psalm 23:5
"The Lord is our Shepherd"

KJV: Thou preparest a table before me in the presence of mine enemies: thou anointest my head with oil; my cup runneth over.

NISV: You prepare a table before me in the presence of my enemies. You anoint my head with oil; my cup overflows.

GNB: You prepare a banquet for me, where all my enemies can see me; you welcome me as an honored guest and fill my cup to the brim.

TMB: You serve me a six-course dinner right in front of my enemies. You revive my drooping head; my cup brims with blessing.

The bad things that happen to us and around us are sometimes hard to comprehend. Jesus doesn't promise everything will be "smooth sailing," but we know that Jesus is with us. He will help us solve our problems and help us through any circumstance. He will see us through and bless us more than we can imagine.

How often do you count your blessings?

january 6

Psalm 23:6
"The Lord is Our Shepherd"

KJV: Surely goodness and mercy shall follow me all the days of my life: and I will dwell in the house of the LORD for ever.

NISV: Surely goodness and love will follow me all the days of my life, and I will dwell in the house of the LORD forever.

GNB: I know that your goodness and love will be with me all my life; and your house will be my home as long as I live.

TMB: Your beauty and love chase after me every day of my life. I'm back home in the house of God for the rest of my life.

Your promises tell us that You will be with us as long as we live. You show us daily the beauty of Your creation. We feel Your love surround us every day. Thank You for the promise that we will come to live with You forever.

See two versions of the 23rd Psalm below.

The King James Version of the Bible seems to have the easiest flow for memorizing. The Message Bible version gives a new perspective. Memorizing scripture is a great way to have the Bible's knowledge at hand whenever you need it. I recommend memorizing as much scripture as possible.

The King James Version of the 23rd Psalm

The Lord is my shepherd; I shall not want. He maketh me to lie down in green pastures: he leadeth me beside the still waters. He restoreth my soul: he leadeth me in the paths of righteousness for his name's sake. Yea, though I walk through the valley of the shadow of death, I will fear no evil: for thou art with me; thy rod and they staff they comfort me. Thou preparest a table before me in the presence of mine enemies: thou anointest my head with oil; my cup runneth over. Surely goodness and mercy shall follow me all the days of my life: and I will dwell in the house of the Lord forever.

The Message Version of the 23rd Psalm

God, my shepherd! I don't need a thing. You have bedded me down in lush meadows, you find me quiet pools to drink from. True to your word, you let me catch my breath and send me in the right direction. Even when the way goes through Death Valley. I'm not afraid when you walk at my side. Your trusty shepherd's crook makes me feel secure. You serve me a six-course dinner right in front of my enemies. You revive my dropping head; my cup brims with blessing. Your beauty and love chase after me every day of my life. I'm back home in the house of God for the rest of my life.

january 7

Acts 4:11-12
Do you have a foundation to build on and stand on?

KJV: This is the stone which was set at nought of you builders which has become the head of the corner. ¹² Neither is there salvation in any other: for there is none other name under heaven given among men, whereby we must be saved.

NISV: He is "'the stone you builders rejected, which has become the capstone.' Salvation is found in no one else, for there is no other name under heaven given to men by which we must be saved."

GNB: Jesus is the one of whom the scripture says, "'The stone that you the builders despised turned out to be the most important of all.' Salvation is to be found through him alone; in all the world there is no one else whom God has given who can save us."

TMB: "Jesus is the stone you masons threw out, which is now the cornerstone. Salvation comes no other way; no other name has been or will be given to us by which we can be saved, only this one."

Jesus is our cornerstone. He will give us the most firm foundation. He cannot be moved.
   Is your foundation formed by the world or the Bible?

january 8

James 5:13-14
Is God with you in all things?

KJV: Is any among you afflicted? Let him pray. Is any merry? Let him sing psalms. ¹⁴ Is any sick among you? Let him call for the elders of the church; and let them pray over him, anointing him with oil in the name of the Lord.

NISV: Is any one of you in trouble? He should pray. Is anyone happy? Let him sing songs of praise. ¹⁴ Is any one of you sick? He should call the elders of the church to pray over him and anoint him with oil in the name of the Lord.

GNB: Is anyone among you in trouble? He should pray. Is anyone happy? He should sing praises. ¹⁴ Is there anyone who is sick? He should send for the church elders, who will pray for and rub olive oil on him in the name of the Lord.

TMB: Are you hurting? Pray. Do you feel great? Sing. Are you sick? Call the church leaders together to pray and anoint you with oil in the name of the Master. Believing-prayer will heal you.

Sometimes it is comforting to know that the words of the Bible from the King James to The Message version really don't change that much. God helps us find the best way to do something and then helps us to do it.

Can you think of a time when praying helped give you a new perspective on the situation?

To keep track of your prayers, make a prayer box by putting a slit in the top of a box. Decorate the box if you like. Write down your prayer requests on a slip of paper and put them in the box. Check it weekly or monthly and see how your prayers are being answered.

january 9

Proverbs 17:22
What kind of an attitude do you have?

KJV: A Merry heart doeth good *like* medicine but a broken spirit drieth the bones.

NISV: A cheerful heart is good medicine, but a crushed spirit dries up the bones.

GNB: Being cheerful keeps you healthy. It is slow death to be gloomy all the time.

TMB: A cheerful disposition is good for your health; gloom and doom leave you bone-tired.

God has given us free will to do what we please. Spending time in prayer and communication with God will help our attitude. Take time to talk to God just like you take time to talk to your friends. He will always listen and give the best answers. You may call on Him anytime of the day or night. He won't hang up on you or tell you it's too late to call.

Where do you look for happiness?

january 10

Proverbs 1:7
Whom do you fear?

KJV: The fear of the Lord is the beginning of knowledge: but fools despise wisdom and instruction.

NISV: The fear of the Lord is the beginning of knowledge, but fools despise wisdom and discipline.

GNB: To have knowledge, you must first have reverence for the Lord. Stupid people have no respect for wisdom and refuse to learn.

TMB: Fresh wisdom to probe and penetrate, the rhymes and reasons of wise men and women.

The foolish cannot understand God's word. It is through reverence and study that we learn about Him. Our wisdom, knowledge, and hope come from the Lord; only when we acknowledge Him as Lord can He help straighten out our lives.

Are you memorizing any scriptures?

january 11

Proverbs 3:1-2
Do you pay attention and live by God's laws?

KJV: My son, forget not my law; but let thine heart keep my commandments: For length of days, and long life, and peace, shall they add to thee.

NISV: My son, do not forget my teaching, but keep my commands in your heart, ² for they will prolong your life many years and bring you prosperity.

GNB: Son, don't forget what I teach you. Always remember what I tell you to do. ² My teaching will give you a long and prosperous life.

TMB: *Don't assume you know it all.* Good friend, don't forget all I've taught you; take to heart my commands. They'll help you live a long, long time, a long life lived full and well.

We can plan how to react in certain situations when we plan for the future. For instance, if you are young and haven't had experience going on a date, talk to your parents or pastor about guidelines of proper behavior. Have in your mind what you will do before you get into a problem. Know what you expect from yourself and how it might affect your future. Will you be happy about your behavior the next day, week, or month, or will you regret something you did in haste the rest of your life? God has everything we need; rely on His word. His teaching and grace will see us through.

choose your destiny

Write about an experience you have had where you wish you had planned ahead. What do you need to plan for now?

january 12

John 3:16
Do you have a friend that would give his life for you?

KJV: For God so loved the world, that he gave his only begotten Son, that whosoever believeth in him should not perish but have everlasting life.

NISV: For God so loved the world that he gave his one and only Son, that whoever believes in him shall not perish but have eternal life.

GNB: For God loved the world so much that he gave his only Son, so that everyone who believes in him may not die but have eternal life.

TMB: "This is how much God loved the world: He gave his Son, his one and only Son. And this is why: so that no one need be destroyed; by believing in him, anyone can have a whole and lasting life."

God has given us His most precious gift, His Son Jesus Christ. Have you experienced what Jesus Christ can do for you? All you need to do is ask Jesus to come into your heart and take away your sins. Just tell Him you will believe and trust in Him. What a difference you will see in your life. Jesus is looking for a relationship with you. Jesus will send the Holy Spirit to strengthen you. Listen to His voice!

I love the song "No One Ever Cared for Me Like Jesus." It says in the second verse:

"Jesus placed His strong and loving arms about me, And He led me in the way I ought to go. No one ever cared for me like Jesus, There's no other friend so kind as He; No one else could take the sin and darkness from me, O how much He cared for me." ("No One Ever Cared for Me Like Jesus" words and music C.F. Weigle.)

Do you know anyone that can take care of you like this? Turn your life over to Jesus.

He is the only one that really cares about you all the time.

january 13

1 John 5:13
By accepting Jesus as our Savior we will have eternal life.

KJV: These things have I written unto you that believe on the name of the Son of God; that ye may know that ye have eternal life, and that ye may believe on the name of the Son of God.

NISV: I write these things to you who believe in the name of the Son of God so that you may know that you have eternal life.

GNB: I am writing this to you so that you may know that you have eternal life-you that believe in the Son of God.

TMB: My purpose in writing is simply this: that you who believe in God's Son will know beyond the shadow of a doubt that you have eternal life, the reality and not the illusion.

It is this simple, no frills attached. God's teaching and grace will help you learn what you need to know. If you don't go to church, find a church that teaches from the Bible. Interview some pastors, ask them if the they believe in Jesus as their Savior. If they say they don't believe that Jesus died to save us from our sins, find another place to worship. It doesn't matter how sincere they seem, if they don't believe Jesus died for our sins and rose again, leave and find a church that teaches from the Bible.

What has been your experience with finding a church you feel comfortable attending?

january 14

John 14:27
Do you have peace in your heart and soul?

- KJV: "Peace I leave with you, my peace I give unto you": not as the world giveth, give I unto you. Let not your heart be troubled, neither let it be afraid.
- NISV: "Peace I leave with you; my peace I give you. I do not give to you as the world gives. Do not let your hearts be troubled and do not be afraid.
- GNB: "Peace is what I leave with you; it is my own peace that I give you. I do not give it as the world does. Do not be worried and upset; do not be afraid.
- TMB: Peace. I don't leave you the way you're used to being left—feeling abandoned, bereft. So don't be upset. Don't be distraught.

The world is always in turmoil. It does not know peace. "To know God is to know peace" (unknown author). If you do not have a relationship with Jesus, God's Son, you will not find peace. Let go of the big "I" and trust Jesus.

january 15

Ephesians 1:7-8
How can we measure the depth of God's love and grace?

KJV: In whom [Christ] we have redemption through his blood, the forgiveness of sins, according to the riches of his grace; ⁸ Where-in he hath abounded toward us in all wisdom and prudence;

NISV: In him [Christ] we have redemption through his blood, the forgiveness of sins, in accordance with the riches of God's grace ⁸ that he lavished on us with all wisdom and understanding.

GNB: For by the death of Christ [and through his blood] we are set free, that is, our sins are forgiven. How great is the grace of God, ⁸ which he gave to us in such large measure!

TMB: Because of the sacrifice of the Messiah, his blood poured out on the altar of the Cross, we're a free people-free of penalties and punishments chalked up by all our misdeeds. And not just barely free, either. *Abundantly* free!

Through Christ's blood and grace, He has forgiven our sins. His spirit is everywhere, and His love protects and surrounds us. He sends the Holy Spirit to comfort us.

Browse the website www.Godtube.org to find more information about the Bible.

january 16

1 John 1:7, 9
What can the blood of Christ do for you?

KJV: But if we walk in the light, as he is in the light, we have fellowship with one another, and the blood of Jesus Christ his Son cleanseth us from all sin…⁹ If we confess our sins, he is faithful and just to forgive us our sins, and to cleanse us from all unrighteousness.

NISV: But if we walk in the light, as he is in the light, we have fellowship with one another, and the blood of Jesus, his Son, purifies us from all sin…⁹ If we confess our sins, he is faithful and just and will forgive us our sins and purify us from all unrighteousness.

GNB: But if we live in the light—… then we have fellowship with one another, and the blood of Jesus, his Son, purifies us from every sin…⁹ But if we confess our sins to God, he will keep his promise and do what is right: he will forgive us our sins and purify us from all our wrongdoing.

TMB: But if we walk in the light, God himself being the light, we also experience a shared life with one another, as the sacrificed blood of Jesus, God's Son, purges all our sin.…⁹ On the other hand, if we admit our sins—make a clean breast of them—he won't let us down; he'll be true to himself. He'll forgive our sins and purge us of all wrongdoing.

Jesus has cleansed us by the blood He shed on the cross. We can pray for His blood to cover us and keep us from harm. When you are distressed and feel the "evil one" is on your doorstep, ask Jesus to cover "Satan" with His blood. The devil cannot compete with the blood that Jesus has shed for us; Satan will leave as quickly as he came.

january 17

Romans 8:28
If God is for us, who can be against us?
He will always be there for us.

KJV: And we know that all things work together for good to them that love God, to them who are the called according to *his* purpose.

NISV: And we know that in all things God works for the good of those who love him, who have been called according to his purpose.

GNB: We know that in all things God works for good with those who love him, those whom he has called according to his purpose.

TMB: He knows us far better than we know ourselves, knows our pregnant condition, and keeps us present before God. That's why we can be so sure that every detail in our lives of love for God is worked into something good.

If we accept God's spirit and word, He will give us His grace and blessing.

If you are curious about the Bible, it is easy to read through in a year. Read three chapters a day. You will be amazed how many things in our lives come from the Bible. It contains almost every law we have in our society. Set a goal, read a few chapters a day. What knowledge you will gain! It is also a good time to memorize scripture.

january 18

Matthew 19:14
How do you treat children?

The disciples were trying to make the children go away and not bother Jesus, but He wanted the children to know that they were very special to Him.

KJV: But Jesus said, "Suffer little children, and forbid them not, to come unto me; for of such is the kingdom of heaven."

NISV: Jesus said, "Let the little children come to me, and do not hinder them, for the kingdom of heaven belongs to such as these."

GNB: Jesus said, "Let the children come to me and do not stop them, because the Kingdom of Heaven belongs to such as these."

TMB: Jesus intervened: "Let the children alone, don't prevent them from coming to me. God's kingdom is made up of people like these."

We all come to Jesus as children. He accepts us as we are, and we can have new birth in Christ Jesus.

There is a web site for children that may give you some ideas for teaching them about Jesus: www.discoveryclub.org.

january 19

Luke 10:37
Who is your neighbor?

In the parable of the Good Samaritan, a teacher of the law asked Jesus, "What must I do to receive eternal life?" Jesus asked him what the scriptures said about this. The man answered, "Love the Lord your God with all your heart, with all; your soul, with all your strength, and with all your mind" and "love your neighbor as yourself" (Luke 10:37, GNB). Jesus said to obey these laws. The man then asked Jesus who his neighbor was. Jesus told him the story of the men who walked past the man who had been attacked by robbers. The first two ignored the injured man, but the Samaritan took pity on him and took care of him. (The injured man was a Levite.)

Jesus asked the people which person they thought was their neighbor.

KJV: And he said, He that shewed mercy on him. Then said Jesus unto him, "Go, and do thou likewise."

NISV: The expert in the law replied, "The one who had mercy on him." Jesus told him, "Go and do likewise."

GNB: The teacher of the Law answered, "The one who was kind to him." Jesus replied, "You go, then and do the same."

TMB: "The one who treated him kindly," the religious scholar responded. Jesus said, "Go and do the same."

How do we treat our neighbors? How can we learn to love and help them?

january 20

John 14:15-17a
When Jesus left His disciples and friends,
He gave them a promise: I will not be
with you in body but in spirit.

KJV: "If ye love me, keep my commandments. ¹⁶ And I will pray the Father, and he shall give you another Comforter, that he may abide with you forever. ¹⁷ Even the Spirit of truth; whom the world cannot receive"—

NISV: If you love me, you will obey what I command. ¹⁶ And I will ask the Father, and he will give you another Counselor to be with you forever. ¹⁷ The Spirit of truth. The world cannot accept him—

GNB: If you love me you will obey my commandments. ¹⁶ I will ask the Father, and he will give you another Helper, who will stay with you forever. ¹⁷ He is the Spirit, who reveals the truth about God. The world cannot receive him, because it cannot see him or know him—

TMB: If you love me, show it by doing what I've told you. I will talk to the Father, and he'll provide you another Friend so that you will always have someone with you. This Friend is the Spirit of Truth. The godless world can't take him in because it doesn't have eyes to see him, doesn't know what to look for. But you know him already because he has been staying with

you, and will even be in you! [When you trust the
LORD, you will feel the Spirit of the LORD, and he
will guide you.]

Have you tried to explain Jesus or the Holy Spirit to someone? They cannot understand the peace God will send through the Holy Spirit until they pray and accept God's forgiveness and ask Him to come into their heart and save them from their sins. By studying our Bible, we will learn what to tell our friends. (John 3:16 and Romans 8:8–28.)

january 21

Romans 8:38–39
What do you think can separate you from the love of God?

KJV: For I am persuaded, that neither death, nor life, nor angels, nor principalities, nor powers, nor things present, nor things to come [39] Nor height, nor depth, nor any other creature, shall be able to separate us from the love of God, which is in Christ Jesus our Lord.

NISV: For I am convinced that neither death nor life, neither angels nor demons, neither the present nor the future, nor any powers, [39] neither height nor depth, nor anything else in all creation, will be able to separate us from the love of God that is in Christ Jesus our Lord.

GNB: For I am certain that nothing can separate us from his love: neither death nor life, neither angels, nor other heavenly rulers of powers, neither the present nor the future. [39] neither the world above nor the world below—there is nothing in all creation that will ever be able to separate us from the love of God which is ours through Christ Jesus our Lord.

TMB: I'm absolutely convinced that nothing—nothing living or dead, angelic or demonic, today or tomorrow; high or low, thinkable or unthinkable—absolutely *nothing* can get between us and God's love because of the way that Jesus our Master has embraced us.

Paul gives us the assurances of God's love. Who else under heaven can make any of these promises except the Lord?

You are the only one that can separate yourself from the love of God by choosing not to follow Him.

january 22

Romans 12:2
Can you live as the rest of the world lives and still be a dedicated member of God's family?

KJV: And be not conformed to this world: but be ye transformed by the renewing of your mind, that ye may prove what is that good, and acceptable, and perfect, will of God.

NISV: Do not conform any longer to the pattern of this world, but be transformed by the renewing of; your mind. Then you will be able to test and approve what God's will is—his good, pleasing and perfect will.

GNB: Do not conform yourselves to the standards of this world, but let God transform you inwardly by a complete change of your mind. Then you will be able to know the will of God-what is good and is pleasing to him and is perfect.

TMB: Don't become so well-adjusted to your culture that you fit into it without even thinking. Instead, fix your attention on God. You'll be changed from the inside out. Readily recognize what he wants from you, and quickly respond to it. Unlike the culture around you, always dragging you down to its level of immaturity, God brings the best out of you, develops well-formed maturity in you.

Paul tells us that we need to be separate from the things of the world to see what Christ has for us. If we believe Christ died for us and we will trust Him, we need to let Him do His work in our hearts and lives. Just let go and let God lead the way. Your destiny will be with the Lord.

january 23

1 Thessalonians 5:3
Where do you find peace?

KJV: For when they shall say, Peace and safety; then sudden destruction cometh upon them, as travail upon a woman with child; and they shall not escape.

NISV: While people are saying, "Peace and safety," destruction will come on them suddenly, as labor pains on a pregnant woman, and they will not escape.

GNB: When people say, "Everything is quiet and safe," then suddenly destruction will hit them! It will come as suddenly as the pains that come upon a woman in labor, and people will not escape.

TMB: About the time everybody's walking around complacently, congratulating each other—"We've sure got it made! Now we can take it easy!"—suddenly everything will fall apart. It's going to come as suddenly and inescapably as birth pangs to a pregnant woman.

Today's world is so uncertain. The terrorists' hidden agenda and cunning are frightening. But their evil deeds will be nothing compared to what the Lord has in store for those who have refused Him at His returning. Is the Lord giving you peace about your future? Are you ready to have peace and safety with the Lord? Just ask Him to come into your heart. He will accept you into His family. Just trust in Him.

Where do you find peace?

january 24

Isaiah 55:8
Can we know the mind of God?

KJV: For my thoughts *are* not your thoughts, neither *are* your ways my ways, saith the Lord.

NISV: "For my thoughts are not your thoughts, neither are your ways my ways," declares the Lord.

GNB: "My thoughts," says the Lord, "are not like yours, and my ways are different from yours."

TMB: "I don't think the way you think. The way you work isn't the way I work." God's Decree.

By listening to God and reading His word, we can find out what He wants us to know.

If you could meet Jesus in person, what would you ask Him?

Dr. Charles Stanley, the television minister, has many good books about prayer. Check his website: www.intouch.org.

january 25

Romans 10:10–11
If you haven't accepted Jesus as your Savior, what do you think you need to do to become a child of God?

KJV: For with the heart man believeth unto righteousness; and with the mouth confession is made unto salvation. [11] For the scripture saith, Whosoever believeth on him shall not be ashamed.

NISV: For it is with your heart that you believe and are justified, and it is with your mouth that you confess and are saved. [11] As the Scripture says, "Anyone who trusts in him will never be put to shame."

GNB: For it is by our faith that we are put right with God; it is by our confession that we are saved. [11] The scripture says, "Whoever believes in him will not be disappointed."

TMB: You're not "doing" anything; you're simply calling out to God, trusting him to do it for you. That's salvation. With your whole being you embrace God setting things right, and then you say it, right out loud: "God has set everything right between him and me!"

Some people don't accept Jesus as their Savior because they think it is too easy. Some think they have to give up too much. Some have to have the love of God proven to them. God has made it very easy to accept Jesus. Because Jesus took on our sin by dying on the cross, all we need to do is say, "I confess that I am a sinner and I invite Jesus into my heart." Praying each day and having communication with Jesus will give you perfect peace. Then you will have the proof you wanted.

What is the most conflicting thing in your life? Do you think God could help you?

january 26

Jeremiah 29:11
If you disobey laws do you think you can be excused and forgiven?

The Israelites have disobeyed God again and again and many are still in exile. The Lord tells them to work hard and increase in number then He will give Jerusalem back to them. Read His promise to them:

KJV: "For I know the thoughts that I think toward you," saith the LORD, "thoughts of peace, and not of evil, to give you an expected end."

NISV: "For I know the plans I have for you," declares the LORD, "plans to prosper you and not to harm you, plans to give you hope and a future."

GNB: "I alone know the plans I have for you, plans to bring you prosperity and not disaster, plans to bring about the future you hope for."

TMB: I know what I'm doing. I have it all planned out—plans to take care of you, not abandon you, plans to give you the future you hope for.

Today we are seeing the Israelites return to Israel and Jerusalem. Today God is fulfilling His promise, and we pray that His return to this earth will be soon. No matter what it is that you have done to break the law, there is always forgiveness from the Lord. He will always be there waiting for us to accept us into His family. Just pray and confess your sin and ask Him to take all your sin away. Choosing your destiny with God will give you peace. God is our hope.

What path are you choosing? What is your destiny?

january 27

Jeremiah 29:13–14
How long will you trust God?

Can you imagine how terrible it was for the Israelites to be removed from their homeland? The Lord said to listen and obey Him. They wouldn't pay attention then, and I wonder if they are paying attention now? What will happen next?

KJV: And ye shall seek me, and find me, when ye shall search for me with all your heart. ¹⁴ And I will be found of you, saith the LORD: and I will turn away your captivity, and I will gather you from all the nations, and from all the places whither I have driven you, saith the LORD; and I will bring you again into the place whence I caused you to be carried away captive.

NISV: "You will seek me and find me when you seek me with all your heart. ¹⁴ I will be found by you," declares the LORD, "and will bring you back from captivity. I will gather you from all the nations and places where I have banished you." declares the LORD, "and will bring you back to the place from which I carried you into exile."

GNB: You will seek me, and you will find me because you will seek me with all your heart. ¹⁴ Yes, I say you will find me, and I will restore you to your land. I will gather you from every country and from every place to which I have scattered you, and I will bring you back to the land from which I had sent you away into exile. I, the Lord have spoken.'

TMB: When you come looking for me, you'll find me. "Yes, when you get serious about finding me and want it more than anything else, I'll make sure you won't be disappointed." God's Decree. "I'll turn things around for you. I'll bring you back from all the countries into which I drove you"—God's Decree—"bring you home to the place from which I sent you off into exile. You can count on it."

The Lord keeps His promises. Why not trust Him today? He is waiting for you to call to Him; He will answer your prayer.
   What prayer do you want God to answer today?

january 28

Ephesians 2:4-5
Do we give mercy to a friend that has done something wrong to us?

KJV: But God, who is rich in mercy, for his great love wherewith he loved us, Even when we were dead in sins, hath quickened us together with Christ, by grace ye are saved.

NISV: But because of his great love for us, God, who is rich in mercy, [5] made us alive with Christ even when we were dead in transgressions—it is by grace you have been saved.

GNB: But God's mercy is so abundant and his love for us is so great, [5] that while we were spiritually dead in our disobedience he brought us to life with Christ. It is by God's grace that you have been saved.

TMB: …immense in mercy and with an incredible love, he embraced us. He took our sin-dead lives and made us alive in Christ. He did all this on his own, with no help from us!

God knew that as mere humans we could not follow His laws or commandments. And though we have sinned and not pleased God, He has given us the ultimate gift. He sent His son to die for us; His Son's life paid for our sins. Thank you, Lord, for Your love, grace, and mercy.

What is your biggest downfall? Do you think God can help you?

january 29

Ephesians 4:4-6
Do we need other gods in our lives?

kjv: There is one body, and one Spirit, even as ye are called in one hope of your calling, ⁵ One Lord, one faith, one baptism. ⁶ One God and Father of all, who is above all, and through all, and in you all.

nisv: There is one body and one Spirit—just as you were called to one hope when you were called—⁵ one Lord, one faith, one baptism; ⁶ one God and Father of all, who is over all and through all and in all.

gnb: There is one body and one Spirit, just as there is one hope to which God has called you. ⁵ There is one Lord, one faith, one baptism: ⁶ there is one God and Father of all mankind, who is Lord of all, works through all, and is in all.

tmb: You have one Master, one faith, one baptism, one God and Father of all, who rules over all, works through all, and is present in all. Everything you are and think and do is permeated with Oneness.

The trinity is the Father, Son, and Holy Spirit, and they are one body. In this body of Christ through God, He meets all our needs, as He has sent the Holy Spirit to comfort us. We have one faith, one baptism, and one Lord. He sees us and takes care of every detail in our lives if we let Him. God is all we need.

If the God in heaven is not your God; who is your god? Does that god give you peace?

january 30

I John 5:5, 11–12
Do you believe that in Jesus' death there
is victory over death and the world?

KJV: Who is he that overcometh the world, but he that believeth that Jesus is the Son of God?…[11] And this is the record, that God hath given to us eternal life, and this life is in his Son. [12] He that hath the Son hath life; and he that hath not the Son of God hath not life.

NISV: Who is it that overcomes the world? Only he who believes that Jesus is the Son of God…[11] And this is the testimony: God has given us eternal life, and this life is in his Son. [12] He who has the Son has life; he who does not have the Son of God does not have life.

GNB: Who can defeat the world? Only the person who believes that Jesus is the Son of God…[11] The testimony is this: God has given us eternal life, and this life has its source in his Son. [12] Whoever has the Son has this life; whoever does not have the Son of God does not have life.

TMB: The person who wins out over the world's ways is simply the one who believes Jesus is the Son of God. [11] If we take human testimony at face value, how much more should we be reassured when God gives testimony as he does here, testifying concerning his

Son. Whoever believes in the Son of God inwardly confirms God's testimony. Whoever refuses to believe in effect calls God a liar, refusing to believe God's own testimony regarding his Son. This is the testimony in essence; God gave us eternal life; the life is in his Son. So, whoever has the Son, has life; whoever rejects the Son, rejects life.

God tells us that the way to eternal life is only through His Son who died on the cross. Live your life through Christ and you will receive the everlasting reward of eternal life. (John 3:16 and Matthew 7:7–8.)

To study more about Jesus look at this website: www.billygraham.org.

january 31

Colossians 3:15
Do you have peace in your heart?

KJV: And let the peace of God rule in your hearts, to the which also ye are called in one body; and be ye thankful.

NISV: Let the peace of Christ rule in your hearts, since as members of one body you were called to peace. And be thankful.

GNB: The peace that Christ gives is to guide you in the decisions you make; for it is to this peace that God has called you together in the one body. And be thankful.

TMB: Let the peace of Christ keep you in tune with each other, in step with each other. None of this going off and doing your own thing. And cultivate thankfulness.

God, through Jesus Christ and the Holy Spirit, is the only way to be connected to the body of Christ. It is through this connection that He can give you perfect peace in your heart. We can be thankful that Jesus did this for us when He died on the cross. When you choose to follow Jesus, your destiny will be assured.

Where will your destiny lead you?

february 1

Romans 3:22-24
Are there a special few that will get into heaven because of good works or good looks?

KJV: Even the righteousness of God *which is* by faith of Jesus Christ unto all and upon all them that believe: for there is no difference: [23] For all have sinned, and come short of the glory of God; [24] Being justified freely by his grace through the redemption that is in Christ Jesus:

NISV: This righteousness from God comes through faith in Jesus Christ to all who believe. There is no difference, [23] for all have sinned and fall short of the glory of God, [24] and are justified freely by his grace through the redemption that came by Christ Jesus.

GNB: God puts people right through their faith in Jesus Christ, God does this to all who believe in Christ, because there is no difference at all: [23] everyone has sinned and is far away from God's saving presence. [24] But by the free gift of God's grace all are put right with him through Christ Jesus, who sets them free.

TMB: The God setting-things-right that we read about has become Jesus-setting-things-right for us. And not only for us, but for everyone who believes in him. For there is no difference between us and them in this. Since we've compiled this long and sorry record as sinners (both us and them) and proved that we are utterly incapable of living the glorious lives God wills for us, God did it for us. Out of sheer generosity he put us in right standing with himself. A pure gift. He got us out of the mess we're in and restored us to where he always wanted us to be. And he did it by means of Jesus Christ.

Jesus says, we all have sinned and cannot be saved unless we ask forgiveness for our sins and accept the grace that God gives us. Jesus is our hope for eternal life.

Have you been forgiven? Have you accepted His love and grace?

february 2

1 Chronicles 4:10
Do you ever ask the Lord for help?

KJV: And Jabez called on the God of Israel, saying, Oh that thou wouldest bless me indeed, and enlarge my coast, and that thine hand might be with me, and that thou wouldest keep me from evil, that it may not grieve me! And God granted him that which he requested.

NISV: Jabez cried out to the God of Israel, "Oh, that you would bless me and enlarge my territory! Let your hand be with me, and keep me from harm so that I will be free from pain." And God granted his request.

GNB: But Jabez prayed to the God of Israel, "Bless me, God, and give me much land. Be with me and keep me from anything evil that might cause me pain." And God gave him what he prayed for.

TMB: Jabez prayed to the God of Israel: "Bless me, O bless me! Give me land, large tracts of land: And provide your personal protection-don't let evil hurt me." God gave him what he asked.

Jabez was a direct descendant of David. God was very evident in his life. We may not be direct descendants of David, but because of God's promises, we know the Lord will bless us when we ask for His help.

What is the most important thing you would like God to give you?

february 3

Colossians 3:1–2
Are you ever confused about what is right and what is wrong?

KJV: If ye then be risen with Christ, seek those things which are above, where Christ sitteth on the right hand of God. ² Set your affection on things above, not on things on the earth.

NISV: Since, then, you have been raised with Christ, set your hearts on things above, where Christ is seated at the right hand of God. ² Set your minds on things above, not on earthly things.

GNB: You have been raised to life with Christ, so set your hearts on the things that are in heaven where Christ sits on his throne at the right side of God. ² Keep your minds fixed on things there, not on things here on earth.

TMB: So if you're serious about living this new resurrection life with Christ, act like it. Pursue the things over which Christ presides. Don't shuffle along, eyes to the ground, absorbed with the things right in front of you. Look up, and be alert to what is going on around Christ—that's where the action is. See things from his perspective.

Trust the Lord Jesus to lead you. Choose the best way to live. When we dwell on earthly things (money, drinking, fooling around, etc.), we find no lasting satisfaction. If we let God through Jesus take our lives and give us things that are of heaven, not earth, we will feel His peace and joy. He will give our lives fulfillment and eternal life. People who have never tried Jesus cannot know this contentment. It is easy for them to know Him. All they need to do is ask Him to come into their life and forgive them of their sins. Talk to a friend today and tell them your experience with God. Show your friends how to find their destiny with God.

february 4

1 Timothy 4:4–5
Let us be thankful to God who created us.

KJV: For every creature of God is good and nothing to be refused, if it be received with thanksgiving: ⁵ For it is sanctified by the word of God and prayer.

NISV: For everything God created is good, and nothing is to be rejected if it is received with thanksgiving ⁵ because it is consecrated by the word of God and prayer.

GNB: Everything that God has created is good; nothing is to be rejected, but everything is to be received with a prayer of thanks, ⁵ because the word of God and the prayer make it acceptable to God.

TMB: Everything God created is good, and to be received with thanks. Nothing is to be sneered at and thrown out. God's Word and our prayers make every item in creation holy.

The Bible tells us that God brought this world into being. Everything that God created was put on earth for us to enjoy. When we believe in God, He asks that we give thanks for all that He has given us. And He will bless us with His miracles. We are put on earth to worship and thank God. God is our hope for eternal life!

What creation theory do you embrace: Intelligent Design or Evolution?

february 5

Proverbs 28:13
Do you think you can hide your sins?

- KJV: He that covereth his sins shall not prosper: but whoso confesseth and forsaketh *them* shall have mercy.
- NISV: He who conceals his sins does not prosper, but whoever confesses and renounces them find mercy.
- GNB: You will never succeed in life if you try to hide your sins. Confess them and give them up; then God will show you mercy.
- TMB: You can't whitewash your sins and get by with it; you find mercy by admitting and leaving them.

We can try to cover up our sins, but God knows the truth and so does our heart. Your sins will catch up with you in the end. Make it easy on yourself and confess your sins. God will remove your sins as far as the east is from the west. Let go and let God show you His love, joy, and peace. See Psalm 103:12.

february 6

Psalm 96:1-2
Can you sing to the Lord even on bad days?

KJV: O Sing unto the LORD a new song: sing unto the LORD, all the earth. ² Sing unto the LORD, bless his name; shew forth his salvation from day to day.

NISV: Sing to the LORD a new song; sing to the LORD, all the earth. ² Sing to the LORD, praise his name; proclaim his salvation day after day.

GNB: Sing a new song to the LORD! Sing to the LORD, all the world! ² Sing to the LORD, and praise him! Proclaim every day the good news that he has saved us.

TMB: Sing God a brand-new song! Earth and everyone in it, sing! Sing to God—*worship* God!

When we sing praises to the Lord, like David, and worship God in joyful songs, we let the Lord know we love Him.

What do you sing as you drive along in your car? You might use your driving time to sing praises to the Lord.

february 7

Psalm 57:1-2
David was in great trouble: Saul was chasing him. David knew the only way he would survive was for the Lord to save him.

KJV: Be merciful unto me, O God, be merciful unto me: for my soul trusteth in thee: yea, in the shadow of they wings will I make my refuge, until *these* calamities be overpast. ² I will cry unto God most high; unto God that performeth all things for me.

NISV: Have mercy on me, O God, have mercy on me, for in you my soul takes refuge. I will take refuge in the shadow of your wings until the disaster has passed. ² I cry out to God Most High, to God, who fulfills his purpose for me.

GNB: Be merciful to me, O God, be merciful, because I come to you for safety. In the shadow of your wings I find protection until the raging storms are over. ² I call to God, the Most High, to God, who supplies my every need.

TMB: Be good to me, God—and now! I've run to you for dear life. I'm hiding out under your wings until the hurricane blows over. I call out to High God, the God who holds me together.

The Lord will be merciful to us and will supply needs that we don't even know we have.

Can you think of something that you really needed that God gave you even though you didn't pray about it?

If you don't have a prayer box, get a box and cut a hole in the top. Decorate the box if you like. Write down your prayer requests on a slip of paper and put them in the box. Check it weekly or monthly and see how your prayers are being answered.

february 8

Colossians 3:17
Do your words and deeds reflect your inner thoughts?

KJV: And whatsoever ye do in word or deed, do all in the name of the LORD Jesus, giving thanks to God and the Father by him.

NISV: And whatever you do, whether in word or deed, do it all in the name of the LORD Jesus, giving thanks to God the Father through him.

GNB: Everything you do or say, then, should be done in the name of the LORD Jesus, as you give thanks through him to God the Father.

TMB: Let every detail in your lives—words, actions, whatever—be done in the name of the Master, Jesus, thanking God the Father every step of the way.

Remember to thank the Lord for everything He gives to us. Talking to Him and thanking Him will help us to keep in touch.

What are you most thankful for?

When Jesus is our Savior and mentor, we don't need movie stars, pop singers, or television personalities to be our heroes. These people can fail and will rarely live up to our expectations. God will fill all our empty longings with His love and never let us down. We can always look up to Him.

february 9

John 15:1-2, 4b
During hurricanes, many trees and branches are torn down and blown away. Have you ever felt like you have been separated from the main life-giving source of God's tree?

KJV: I *Am* the true vine, and my Father is the husbandman. ² Every branch in me that beareth not fruit he taketh away: and every branch that beareth fruit, he purgeth it, that it may bring forth more fruit. ⁴...As the branch cannot bear fruit of itself, except it abide in the vine; no more can ye, except ye abide in me.

NISV: "I am the true vine, and my Father is the gardener. ² He cuts off every branch in me that bears no fruit, while every branch that does bear fruit he prunes so that it will be even more fruitful. ⁴...No branch can bear fruit by itself; it must remain in the vine. Neither can you bear fruit unless you remain in me.

GNB: I am the real vine, and my Father is the gardener. ² He breaks off every branch in me that does not bear fruit, and he prunes every branch that does bear fruit, so that it will be clean and bear more fruit. ⁴...A branch cannot bear fruit by itself; it can do so only if it remains in the vine. In the same way you cannot bear fruit unless you remain me.

TMB: I am the Real Vine and my Father is the Farmer.

He cuts off every branch of me that doesn't bear grapes. And every branch that is grape-bearing he prunes back so it will bear even more. [4]..."Live in me. Make your home in me just as I do in you. In the same way that a branch can't bear grapes by itself but only by being joined to the vine you can't bear fruit unless you are joined with me."

We can only bring other people into the fellowship of God's love if we are firmly attached to the main source of God's food, the Bible.

If you would like to look at a web site for information on how to become connected to the tree of life, try www.lifesgreatestquestion.com/way_home.

february 10

Philippians 4:6-7
Have you ever asked God for something but you didn't really think He was listening to you?

KJV: Be careful for nothing; but in everything by prayer and supplication with thanksgiving let your requests be made know unto God. ⁷ And the peace of God, which passeth all understanding, shall keep your hearts and minds through Christ Jesus.

NISV: Do not be anxious about anything, but in everything, by prayer and petition, with thanksgiving, present your requests to God. ⁷ And the peace of God, which transcends all understanding, will guard your hearts and your minds in Christ Jesus.

GNB: Don't worry about anything, but in all your prayers ask God for what you need, always asking him with a thankful heart. ⁷ And God's peace which is far beyond human understanding, will keep your hearts and minds safe in union with Christ Jesus.

TMB: Don't fret or worry. Instead of worrying, pray. Let petitions and praises shape your worries into prayers, letting God know your concerns. Before you know it, a sense of God's wholeness, everything coming together for good, will come and settle you down. It's wonderful what happens when Christ displaces worry at the center of your life.

God is waiting to hear our requests. He has put us on earth to serve Him. When we serve Him, He listens and helps us understand what is best for us. He will answer our prayers according to His will and show us His love.

When is the last time God answered your prayers?

february 11

Proverbs 29:18
What do you think about removing the words "under God" from our pledge of allegiance?

KJV: Where there is no vision, the people perish: but he that keepeth the law, happy is he.

NISV: Where there is no revelation, the people cast off restraint; but blessed is he who keeps the law.

GNB: A nation without God's guidance is a nation without order. Happy is the man who keeps God's law.

TMB: If people can't see what God is doing, they stumble all over themselves; but when they attend to what he reveals, they are most blessed.

Our country has been so blessed by God that many take it for granted. And some people in the United States are trying to get the phrase, "under God," taken out of our pledge of allegiance. To remove one of the few remaining mentions of God from our presence is frightening and dangerous. (The United States Supreme Court did strike down the first attempt to get it removed.) However the man who started the first lawsuit has filed new papers in California's ninth district court to attack the pledge again. The people in our country need to pray that God will be our protector and strength.

And if we don't pledge any allegiance to God, why should He pay any attention to us and our country?

Do you teach your children to rely on God? If we teach

our children that praying is the best source of strength, when they go to school or leave their home, this source of comfort will always be with them. If we have praying children, we have a better connection to them wherever they go. They should know God is always available not just in time of need, but all hours of the day. God is available in good and in bad situations. Prayer is our "secret weapon." Will we allow it to help shape their destiny?

After the attack on the World Trade Center, some reporters asked Billy Graham why God let the attack happen to America. I am not sure of the exact words, but he basically answered: the people of America have forgotten God. The reporters had no reply.

What are your thoughts on why things happened as they did on 9/11/2001?

february 12

2 Corinthians 3:14-17
Is your mind open to what the Lord has to say to you?

kjv: ¹⁴ But their minds were blinded: for until this day remaineth the same veil untaken away in the reading of the old testament; which *veil* is done away in Christ. ¹⁵ But even unto this day when Moses is read, the veil is upon their heart [people of Israel]. ¹⁶ Nevertheless when it [Israel] shall turn to the Lord, the veil shall be taken away. ¹⁷ Now the Lord is that Spirit: and where the Spirit of the Lord *is,* there *is* liberty.

nisv: ¹⁴ But their minds were made dull, [Israelites] for to this day the same veil remains when the old covenant is read. It has not been removed, because only in Christ is it taken away. ¹⁵ Even to this day when Moses is read, a veil covers their hearts. ¹⁶ But whenever anyone turns to the Lord, the veil is taken away. ¹⁷ Now the Lord is the Spirit, and where the Spirit of the Lord is, there is freedom.

gnb: ¹⁴Their minds, indeed were closed; and to this very day their minds are covered with the same veil as they read the books of the old covenant. The veil is removed only when a person is joined to Christ. ¹⁵ Even today [people of Israel] whenever they read the Law of Moses, the veil still covers their minds.

¹⁶ But it can be removed, [the veil] as scripture says about Moses: "His veil was removed when he turned to the Lord." ¹⁷ Now "the Lord" in this passage is the Spirit; and where the Spirit of the Lord is present, there is freedom.

TMB: Unlike Moses, we have nothing to hide. Everything is out in the open with us. He wore a veil so the children of Israel wouldn't notice that the glory was fading away—and they *didn't* notice. They didn't notice it then and they don't notice it now, don't notice that there's nothing left behind that veil. Even today when the proclamations of that old, bankrupt government are read out, they can't see through it. Only Christ can get rid of the veil so they can see for themselves that there's nothing there. Whenever, though, they turn to face God as Moses did, God removes the veil and there they are face to face! They suddenly recognize that God is a living, personal presence, not a piece of chiseled stone. And when God is personally present, a living Spirit, that old, constricting legislation is recognized as obsolete. We're free of it!

The true secrets of the Bible are hidden from unbelievers. The Lord reveals Himself when we accept and believe in Him and we receive the Holy Spirit of Jesus Christ. If you have a personal relationship with Jesus, He will show you what He wants you to learn in His word.

What is your true agenda or strategic plan for your life? Is it written down?

february 13

Proverbs 27:1-2
Are you the first person to tell everyone how great you are? God tells us:

KJV: Boast not thyself of tomorrow; for thou knowest not what a day may bring forth. ² Let another man praise thee, and not thine own mouth; a stranger, and not thine own lips.

NISV: Do not boast about tomorrow, for you do not know what a day may bring forth. ² Let another praise you, and not your own mouth; someone else, and not your own lips.

GNB: Never boast about tomorrow. You don't know what will happen between now and then. ² Let other people praise you-even strangers; never do it yourself.

TMB: Don't brashly announce what you're going to do tomorrow; you don't know the first thing about tomorrow. ² Don't call attention to yourself; let others do that for you.

About the time we tell someone how great we are, things seem to blow up. You may have greater satisfaction keeping what you have accomplished a secret between you and God. When someone else tells other people what a great job you have done, it makes you a "hero" and it makes you feel great. Don't forget to give God the glory and thanks for helping you accomplish your goals.

When did you last thank God for all He has done for you?

february 14

Psalm 115:1
When we pray, do we give God the glory and respect that He deserves?

- KJV: Not unto us, O Lord, not unto us, but unto thy name give glory, for thy mercy, *and* for thy truth's sake.
- NISV: Not to us, O Lord, not to us but to your name be the glory, because of your love and faithfulness.
- GNB: To you alone, O Lord, to you alone, and not us, must glory be given because of your constant love and faithfulness.
- TMB: Not for our sake, God, no, not for our sake, but for your name's sake, show your glory. Do it on account of your merciful love, do it on account of your faithful ways.

Let us be thankful and give all the glory and honor to God for His faithfulness to us, so He will show us His hope, love, joy, and peace.
How do you thank God?

february 15

Matthew 7:1-2
Do you judge people without thinking how it sounds to others?

KJV: Judge not, that ye be not judged. ² For with what judgment ye judge, ye shall be judged: and with what measure ye mete, it shall be measured to you again.

NISV: Do not judge, or you too will be judged? ² For in the same way you judge others, you will be judged, and with the measure you use, it will be measured to you.

GNB: Do not judge others, so that God will not judge you. ² For God will judge you in the same way you judge others, and he will apply to you the same rules you apply to others.

TMB: Don't pick on people, jump on their failures, and criticize their faults—unless, of course, you want the same treatment. *The* critical spirit has a way of boomeranging.

If we do not know the background of the problem or person, how can we criticize the situation? If we talk about the person, we will only make matters worse. Take the problem to God. He will help the person and help us understand the person with the problem.

What person seems to be the biggest thorn in your life? How do you deal with them?

february 16

James 2:1
Do you find it hard to have respect for people that are different from you or your friends?

KJV: My brethren, have not the faith of our Lord Jesus Christ, the Lord of glory, with respect of persons.

NISV: My brothers, as believers in our glorious Lord Jesus Christ, don't show favoritism.

GNB: My brothers, as believers in our Lord Jesus Christ, the Lord of glory, you must never treat people in different ways according to their outward appearance.

TMB: My dear friends, don't let public opinion influence how you live out our glorious, Christ-originated faith.

Because our world is so diverse, it is hard to give other people and nations the respect due them. Jesus does not look at the outward appearance, geographical location, or social standing of a person, but He looks at their heart. Because we cannot look at their heart and are not supposed to make judgments about people, we should treat everyone the same.

february 17

Romans 5:1
Do we earn our way to heaven with works?

KJV: Therefore being justified by faith, we have peace with God through our Lord Jesus Christ:

NISV: Therefore, since we have been justified through faith, we have peace with God through our Lord Jesus Christ.

GNB: Now that we have been put right with God through faith, we have peace with God through our Lord Jesus Christ.

TMB: By entering through faith into what God has always wanted to do for us—set us right with him, make us fit for him—we have it all together with God because of our Master Jesus.

God's great plan for our lives has given us peace through our faith in Him. Getting involved in a church and doing church work will help us to get to know other believers and help the church. But we cannot earn eternal life by our good deeds. We don't "need" to or "have" to do anything else. God just wants us to confess our sins to Him, live by our faith in Him and trust His word. That is why He sent His son to save us.

What is the plan for your life?

february 18

Isaiah 55:6
Where do you look for things about God?

KJV: Seek ye the LORD while he may be found, call ye upon him while he is near.

NISV: Seek the LORD while he may be found; call on him while he is near.

GNB: Turn to the LORD and pray to him, now that he is near.

TMB: Seek God while he's here to be found, pray to him while he's close at hand.

The things the Lord wants us to know are in the Bible, not from some guru. The real God is as close as a prayer no matter where you are. You don't have to go looking for Him. He is waiting to hear from you about any of your concerns. Just talk to Him. He will listen to you. Ask Him to forgive you of your sins and come into your heart. Ask Him to give you His peace. Visit a local church and get involved. The pastor and people can help you learn more about God.

february 19

Philippians 4:12-13
Is it hard to be content all the time? Do we argue and fight and want more "things"?

KJV: I know both how to be abased, and I know how to abound: every where and in all things I am instructed both to be full and to be hungry, both to abound and to suffer need. ¹³ I can do all things through Christ; which strengtheneth me.

NISV: I know what it is to be in need, and I know what it is to have plenty. I have learned the secret of being content in any and every situation, whether well fed or hungry, whether living in plenty or in want. ¹³ I can do everything through him who gives me strength.

GNB: I know what it is to be in need and what it is to have more than enough. I have learned this secret, so that anywhere, at any time, I am content, whether I am full or hungry, whether I have too much or little. ¹³ I have the strength to face all conditions by the power that Christ gives me.

TMB: I've learned by now to be quite content whatever my circumstances. I'm just as happy with little as with much, with much as with little. I've found the recipe for being happy whether full or hungry, hands full or hands empty. Whatever I have, wherever I am,

I can make it through anything in the One who makes me who I am.

Paul, who lived "a life pleasing to God," went through all kinds of torture, pain, and ridicule. Yet he tells us that Christ gave him the strength to get through prison and all kinds of humiliation. Paul along with Silas trusted in the Lord and sang until the gates of the prison fell open. How great it would be if we could trust Jesus enough to be that kind of witness. Day by day we can grow stronger in our relationship with God through prayer and meditation.

february 20

Psalm 116:1-2, 5-6
Have you ever been in a desperate situation and called to the Lord for help?

KJV: I Love the Lord, because he hath heard my voice and my supplications. ² Because he hath inclined has ear unto me, therefore will I call upon him as long as I live.... ⁵ Gracious is the Lord, and righteous; yea, our God is merciful. ⁶ The Lord preserveth the simple: I was brought low, and he helped me.

NISV: I love the Lord, for he heard my voice; he heard my cry for mercy. ² Because he turned his ear to me, I will call on him as long as I live... ⁵ The Lord is gracious and righteous, our God is full of compassion. ⁶ The Lord protects the simplehearted; when I was in great need, he saved me.

GNB: I love the Lord, because he hears me; he listens to my prayers. ² He listens to me every time I call to him.... ⁵ The Lord is merciful and good; our God is compassionate. ⁶ The Lord protects the helpless; when I was in danger, he saved me.

TMB: I love God because he listened to me, listened as I begged for mercy. He listened so intently as I laid out my case before him.... ⁵ God is gracious—it is he who makes things right, our most compassionate God. God takes the side of the helpless; when I was at the end of my rope, he saved me.

As I was working on this verse, my daughter called. She said her two dogs had run away. It was about 11:00 at night. I prayed that the Lord would help the dogs find their way home or we would find them. My husband and I got in the car to look for them...with no luck. Then my daughter and husband looked for them. One dog came home about 11:30 p.m. without the other dog. About midnight my husband and I started looking again. Later as we were going home, we decided to pray one more time and take one more pass through the neighborhood. Almost immediately my husband spotted a figure bending down looking at something at the side of the road. A man in the neighborhood had been taking a walk and was bending over a little black dog. A car had hit the dog. He said he had found the dog about a half hour before. He went home and came back with some food and water. We were so thankful the Lord had saved our pet and sent someone to look after him.

My daughter and I took the dog to the emergency animal clinic where they x-rayed him. He had a fractured pelvis and some internal injuries. The doctor said his injuries should heal in about six weeks with rest. It would have broken our grandson's heart to have lost his little dog.

Thank you, Lord, for listening and answering our prayers, and for even taking care of our pets. The Lord is waiting for us to call on Him. No matter how big, small, or desperate the problem, He is a compassionate God and is there to help protect us and save us.

february 21

Psalm 136:1
How long does our Lord give us mercy?

KJV: O give thanks unto the LORD for he is good: for his mercy *endureth* forever.

NISV: Give thanks to the LORD, for he is good. *His love endures forever.*

GNB: Give thanks to the LORD, because he is good; his love is eternal.

TMB: Thank God! He deserves your thanks. *His love never quits.*

In Psalm 136 there are twenty-five verses telling us who God is and how His great love and mercy continues. The Lord takes care of us in every way possible, even in ways we can't know or understand. Thank You, Lord, for Your love and care for each one of us. Thank You too for Your help in taking care of people, pets, and the little things we care about.

How is God good to you?

february 22

1 Peter 5:8
Do you feel like you are fighting against unseen evil forces?

KJV: Be sober, be vigilant; because your adversary the devil, as a roaring lion, walketh about, seeking whom he may devour.

NISV: Be self-controlled and alert. Your enemy the devil prowls around like a roaring lion looking for someone to devour.

GNB: Be alert, be on watch! Your enemy, the Devil, roams around like a roaring lion, looking for someone to devour.

TMB: Keep a cool head. Stay alert. The Devil is poised to pounce, and would like nothing better than to catch you napping.

Evil forces are described as the devil. He comes disguised in so many forms: material things, beauty, money, religion, pride, arrogance, lust, and lies. I'm sure you could name many more deceptions. Our world is changing rapidly every day. It is hard to find out what is real and true. As we hold onto the promises of God, we must learn to listen to and trust Him more. Things are not going to get better here on earth. Only He can lead us safely through what is ahead.

Do you think God is trustworthy?

february 23

Psalm 138:3
Where do you get your strength?

KJV: In the day when I cried thou answeredst me, and strengthenedst me *with* strength in my soul.

NISV: When I called, you answered me; you made me bold and stouthearted.

GNB: You answered me when I called to you; with your strength you strengthened me.

TMB: The moment I called out, you stepped in; you made my life large with strength.

If you are depending on your own power and strength to do everything, you may find out one of these days it isn't enough; try turning your trouble over to the Lord. You will feel relieved. He will help you solve your problems in ways that will astound you. Let go of the big "me" and let God take control. God makes all things possible in His strength, not ours.

From where do you get your strength?

Look at http://bible.christianity.com for Bible study.

february 24

Psalm 135:15-18
Are the most important things in life your possessions?

KJV: The idols of the heathen *are* silver and gold, the work of men's hands. ⁶ They have mouths, but they speak not; eyes have they, but they see not; ¹⁷ They have ears, but they hear not, neither is there *any* breath in their mouths. ¹⁸ They that make them are like unto them: so *is* every one that trusteth in them.

NISV: The idols of the nations are silver and gold, made by the hands of men. ¹⁶ They have mouths, but cannot speak, eyes, but they cannot see; ¹⁷ they have ears, but cannot hear, nor is there breath in their mouths. ¹⁸ Those who make them will be like them, and so will all who trust in them.

GNB: The gods of the nations are made of silver and gold: they are formed by human hands. ¹⁶ They have mouths, but cannot speak, and eyes, but cannot see, ¹⁷ They have ears, but cannot hear: they are not even able to breathe. ¹⁸ May all who made them and who trust in them become like the idols they have made!

TMB: The gods of the godless nations are mere trinkets, made for quick sale in the markets: Chiseled mouths that can't talk, painted eyes that can't see. Carved ears that can't hear—dead wood! Cold metal! Those who make and trust them become like them.

If you prayed to a statue, what kind of answer could it give you? What good is a god that you talk to if it doesn't have ears to hear or a voice to speak or a way to answer you? It is so much better to worship the living God. He can respond to you and help you find solutions to your problems.

If you haven't put your trust in the Lord, why not do it now? What can you lose except those empty lonely feelings? God will supply all your needs. He is real, and can be real to you. Just invite Him into your heart by praying this simple prayer: "Lord, I need You. Come into my life and forgive all my sin. I will love and serve You." You can pray this prayer anytime. He is available any hour of the day or night.

He is waiting to hear your voice.

february 25

Luke 17:14-15
Did the Lord take care of something and you took the results for granted?

- KJV: And when he saw them, [The ten lepers said, take pity on us] he said unto them. Go show yourselves unto the priests. And it came to pass, that as they went, they were cleansed. ¹⁵ And one of them, when he saw that he was healed, turned back, and with a loud voice glorified God.

- NISV: When he saw them, [The ten lepers said, take pity on us] "Go, show yourselves to the priest," And as they went, they were cleansed. ¹⁵ One of them, when he saw he was healed, came back, praising God in a loud voice.

- GNB: Jesus saw them [The ten lepers said, take pity on us] and said to them "Go and let the priests examine you." On the way they were made clean. ¹⁵ When one of them saw that he was healed, he came back, praising God in a loud voice.

- TMB Taking a good look at them, he said, "Go, show yourselves to the priests." They went, and while still on their way, became clean. One of them, when he realized that he was healed, turned around and came back, shouting his gratitude, glorifying God.

Only one man out of the ten lepers bothered to thank the Lord. In Luke 17:19 it says the Lord said to the one man who returned to thank Him, "Rise and go: your faith has made you well" (NISV). It does not say the other nine men's leprosy returned, but that is the impression the scripture leaves with us. I wonder what would happen to us if the Lord decided to answer our prayers according to our thanks to Him.

Do you take time to thank the Lord during your busy day?

february 26

Psalm 3:3-4
Do you ever feel totally alone and rejected?

KJV: But, thou, O Lord, art a shield for me; my glory, and the lifter up of mine head. ⁴ I cried unto the Lord with my voice, and he heard me out of his holy hill. Selah

NISV: But you are a shield around me, O Lord; you bestow glory on me and lift up my head. ⁴ To the Lord I cry aloud, and he answers me from his holy hill. *Selah*

GNB: But you, O Lord, are always my shield from danger; you give me victory and restore my courage. ⁴ I call to the Lord for help, and from his sacred hill he answers me.

TMB: But you, God, shield me on all sides; You ground my feet, you lift my head high; With all my might I shout up to God, His answers thunder from the holy mountain.

The Lord can be our shield and protector. His holy hill of Zion represents the strength, hope, love, joy, and peace that only He can give us.

The web site www.tatepublishing.com has many books available on Christian subjects.

february 27

Ephesians 2:8-10
Is it hard to receive gifts?

KJV: For by grace are ye saved through faith; and that not yourselves: *it is* the gift of God: ⁹ Not of works, lest any man should boast. ¹⁰ For we are his workmanship, created in Christ Jesus unto good works, which God hath before ordained that we should walk in them.

NISV: For it is by grace you have been saved, through faith—and this not from yourselves, it is the gift of God ⁹ not by works, so that no one can boast. ¹⁰ For we are God's workmanship, created in Christ Jesus to do good works, which God prepared in advance for us to do.

GNB: For it is by God's grace that you have been saved through faith. It is not the result of your own efforts, but God's gift, ⁹ so that no one can boast about it. ¹⁰ God has made us what we are, and in our union with Christ Jesus he has created us for a life of good deeds, which he has already prepared for us to do.

TMB: Now God has us where he wants us, with all the time in this world and the next to shower grace and kindness upon us in Christ Jesus. Saving is all his idea, and all his work. All we do is trust him enough to let him do it. It's God's gift from start to finish! We don't play the major role. If we did, we'd probably go around bragging that we'd done the whole thing! No, we neither make nor save ourselves. God does both the making and saving. He creates each of us by Christ Jesus to join him in the work he does, the good work he has gotten ready for us to do, work we had better be doing.

The greatest gift is from God; it is eternal life. All the good works we do will help us have full and happy lives, but the good works will not give us eternal life. All we need to do is to call out to God, ask for forgiveness for our sins, and accept the gift, His Son, which He has already given to us by dying on the cross.

To learn more about God's saving grace see Chuck Swindol's website: www.insight.org.

february 28

Psalm 37:23-24
Who is guiding your life?

KJV: The steps of a good man are ordered by the LORD: and he delighteth in his way. ²⁴ Though he fall, he shall not be utterly cast down: for the LORD upholdeth *him with his* hand.

NISV: If the LORD delights in a man's way, he makes his steps firm; ²⁴ though he stumble, he will not fall, for the LORD upholds him with his hand.

GNB: The LORD guides a man in the way he should go and protects those who please him. ²⁴ If they fall, they will not stay down, because the LORD will help them up.

TMB: Stalwart walks in step with God; his path blazed by God, he's happy. If he stumbles, he's not down for long; God has a grip on his hand.

If you trust the Lord to guide your life and you are obeying His word, you can trust Him to be there and to help you through any situation.
　　Read Rick Warren's book *The Purpose Driven Life.*
What is the purpose of your life?

february 29

Lamentations 3:22-24
In what way has the Lord shown you His mercy?

KJV: *It is of* the LORD's mercies that we are not consumed, because his compassions fail not. ²³ *They are* new every morning: great *is* thy faithfulness. ²⁴ The LORD *is* my portion, saith my soul; therefore will I hope in him.

NISV: Because of the LORD's great love we are not consumed, for his compassions never fail. ²³ They are new every morning; great is your faithfulness. ²⁴ I say to my self, "The LORD is my portion; therefore I will wait for him."

GNB: The LORD's unfailing love and mercy still continue, ²³ Fresh as the morning, as sure as the sunrise. ²⁴ The LORD is all I have, and so in him I put my hope.

TMB: God's loyal love couldn't have run out, his merciful love couldn't have dried up. They're created new every morning. How great your faithfulness! I'm sticking with God (I say it over and over), He's all I've got left.

In the chorus of the song "Great Is Thy Faithfulness," it says, "All I have need of thy hands have provided." Lord, thank You for Your compassion and understanding. You do provide for us, You give us more than we ask for.

("Great Is Thy Faithfulness" words, T. O. Chisholm music, William M. Runyan, Published by: Church Service Hymns, The Rodeheaver Hall-Mack Co.)

march 1

Ephesians 4:7, 11-12
What special gift has the Lord given you?

KJV: But unto every one of us is given grace according to the measure of the gift of Christ...¹¹ And he gave some apostles; and some, prophets; some, evangelists; and some, pastors and teachers; ¹² For the perfecting of the saints, for the work of the ministry, for the edifying of the body of Christ;

NISV: But to each one of us grace has been given as Christ apportioned it...¹¹ It was he who gave to some to be apostles, some to be prophets, some to be evangelists, and some to be pastors and teachers, ¹² to prepare God's people for works of service, so that the body of Christ may be built up.

GNB: Each one of us has received a special gift in proportion to what Christ has given...¹¹ It was he who "gave gifts to mankind"; he appointed some to be apostles, others to be to be prophets, others to be evangelists, others to be pastors, and teachers. ¹² He did this to prepare all God's people for the work of Christian service, in order to build up the body of Christ.

TMB: But that doesn't mean you should all look and speak and act the same. Out of the generosity of Christ, each of us is given his own gift...¹¹⁻¹² He handed out gifts above and below, filled heaven with his gifts, filled earth with his gifts. He handed out gifts of apostle, prophet, evangelist, and pastor-teacher to train Christians in skilled servant work, working within Christ's body, the church.

Many times it is hard to witness. Pray that the Lord will help you say the right thing, and you will be amazed at what you will say. Some of us may not have a title in church, but we are all "witnesses" to the people around us. The Lord gives us gifts according to our needs and dedication to Him. Become part of a church, and the people will help you develop your gifts. Our life speaks of who we are more than any words we say.

What gifts would you like to share?

march 2

Matthew 6:7–13
Do you ever have a hard time finding the right words to pray?

It is especially difficult to pray when you are feeling desperate. The Lord's Prayer tells us the best way to communicate with our heavenly Father. Here are the versions from the four translations to guide us.

KJV: But when ye pray, use not vain repetitions...[8]...your Father knoweth what things ye have need of, before ye ask him. [9-13] After this manner therefore pray ye:

"Our Father which art in heaven, Hallowed be thy name. Thy kingdom come, Thy will be done in earth, as *it is* in heaven. Give us this day our daily bread. And forgive us our debts, as we forgive our debtors. And lead us not into temptation, but deliver us from evil: For thine is the kingdom, and the power, and the glory, for ever. Amen

NISV: And when you pray, do not keep on babbling...[8] for your Father knows what you need before you ask...[9] This, then, is how you should pray: [10-13] Our Father in heaven, hallowed be your name, your kingdom come, your will be done on earth as it is in heaven. Give us today our daily bread. Forgive us our debts, as we also have forgiven our debtors, and lead us not into temptation, but deliver us from the evil one.

GNB: "When you pray do not use...meaningless words...[8]

Your Father already knows what you need before you ask him. ⁹ This, then, is how you should pray: ¹⁰⁻¹³ 'Our Father in heaven: May your holy name be honored; may your Kingdom come; may your will be done on earth as it is in heaven. Give us today the food we need. Forgive us the wrongs we have done, as we forgive the wrongs that others have done to us. Do not bring us to hard testing, but keep us safe from the Evil one.'"

TMB: ⁷⁻⁸ The world is full of so-called prayer warriors who are prayer-ignorant. They're full of formulas and programs…Don't fall for that nonsense. This is your Father you are dealing with, and he knows better than you what you need. ⁹ With a God like this loving you, you can pray very simply. Like this: ¹⁰⁻¹³

"Our Father in heaven.
Reveal who you are.
Set the world right;
Do what's best—as above, so below.
Keep us alive with three square meals.
Keep us forgiven with you and forgiving others.
Keep us safe from ourselves and the Devil.
You're in charge!
You can do anything you want!
You're ablaze in beauty! Yes. Yes. Yes."

Rev. Charles L. Allen has written a book called God's Psychiatry. One of the chapters is about the Lord's Prayer. He calls the chapter "How to Talk to God." It is a great read for healing of mind and soul. In it he says "With faith you can work miraculous changes in your life." Just repeating and thinking about the words of the Lord's Prayer will give you strength and guidance every day.

march 3

Philippians 3:7
What do consider valuable?

KJV: [Paul says...] But what things were gain to me, those I counted loss for Christ.

NISV: [Paul says...] But whatever was to my profit I now consider loss for the sake of Christ.

GNB: [Paul says...] But all those things that I might count as profit I now reckon as loss for Christ's sake.

TMB: [Paul says...] The very credentials these people are waving around as something special, I'm tearing up and throwing out with the trash—along with everything else I used to take credit for. And why? because of Christ. Yes, all the things I once thought were so important are gone from my life.

Paul tells us that anything he valued before he found Jesus Christ means nothing to him now. Jesus will fill your heart, mind, and soul with all you need.

To learn more about an abundant life in Christ, look at the web site: http://bible.christianity.com and click on "Bible in a Year."

march 4

2 Corinthians 5:17, 21
Are you or do you want to become a
new creation in Christ Jesus?

(In the verses below, verse 21 appears before verse 17. The asterisk denotes the beginning of verse 17.)

KJV: ²¹ For he hath made him to be sin for us, who knew no sin; that we might be made the righteousness of God in Him. * ¹⁷ Therefore if any man *be* in Christ, *he* is a new creature: old things are passed away; behold, all things are become new.

NISV: ²¹ God made him who had no sin to be sin for us, so that in him we might become the righteousness of God. * ¹⁷ Therefore, if anyone is in Christ, he is a new creation; the old has gone, the new has come!

GNB: ²¹ Christ was without sin, but for our sake God made him share our sin in order that in union with him we might share the righteousness of God. * ¹⁷ When anyone is joined to Christ, he is a new being; the old is gone, and the new has come.

TMB: ²¹ How? You say. In Christ. God put the wrong on him who never did anything wrong, so we could be put right with God. * ¹⁷ He included everyone in his death so that everyone could also be included in his life, a resurrection life, a far better life than people ever lived on their own.

When Christ comes into your life, He gives you a longing for things that are spiritual. This is the "new creation" we are looking for. We will find it through Christ's grace and in His saving power.

Have you experienced a new creation in Jesus?

Read John 3:16.

march 5

Hebrews 6:19-20
When Jesus died on the cross, he gave us the hope of eternal life. His life replaced the sacrifice of ancient days.

KJV: Which *hope* we have as an anchor of the soul, both sure and stedfast, and which entereth into that within the vail; [20] Whither the forerunner is for us entered, *even* Jesus, made an high priest for ever after the order of Melchisedec.

NISV: We have this hope as an anchor for the soul, firm and secure; It enters the inner sanctuary behind the curtain, [20] where Jesus, who went before us, has entered on our behalf. He has become a high priest forever, in the order of Melchizedek.

GNB: We have this hope as an anchor for our lives. It is safe and sure, and goes through the curtain of the heavenly temple into the inner sanctuary. [20] On our behalf Jesus has gone in there before us and has become a high priest forever, as the successor of Melchizedek.

TMB: [We have this hope] It's an unbreakable spiritual life line, reaching past all appearances right to the very presence of God where Jesus, running on ahead of us, has taken up his permanent post as high priest for us, in the order of Melchizedek.

Prior to Jesus dying on the cross, no one could pass beyond the sacred veil in the temple. Only the high priest could pass through the veil to the holy of holies. This is where sacrifices were presented to God. We do not have to make animal or other sacrifices to God anymore. because God sent us the gift of His Son Jesus to die on the cross to be the sacrifice for our sins. Read John 3:16.

Have you accepted the gift God sent to you?

march 6

Hebrews 12:12–14
Do we follow the instructions God has set out for us?

KJV: Wherefore lift up the hands which hang down, and the feeble knees; ¹³ And make straight paths for your feet, lest that which is lame be turned out of the way but let it rather be healed. ¹⁴ Follow peace with all *men,* and holiness, without which no man shall see the Lord:

NISV: Therefore, strengthen your feeble arms and weak knees. ¹³ Make level paths for your feet, so that the lame may not be disabled, but rather healed. ¹⁴ Make every effort to live in peace with all men and to be holy; without holiness no one will see the Lord.

GNB: Lift up your tired hands, then, and strengthen your trembling knees! ¹³ Keep walking on straight paths, so that the lame foot may not be disabled, but instead be healed. ¹⁴ Try to be at peace with everyone, and try to live a holy life, because no one will see the Lord without it.

TMB: So don't sit around on your hands! No more dragging your feet! Clear the path for long-distance runners so no one will trip and fall, so no one will step in a hole and sprain an ankle. Help each other out. And run for it! Work at getting along with each other and with God. Otherwise you'll never get so much as a glimpse of God.

We need to take care of our bodies. If we don't, our minds cannot comprehend anything. We need to do our part by physically exercising our bodies just like we exercise our minds by reading. In exercising, we keep the body moving to make it grow stronger. The Lord will give strength to our minds to help us live peaceably with our fellow man. We influence everyone around us when we follow the instructions given by the Lord.

Do you take time to exercise?

For a simple exercise plan visit www.pilates.com

march 7

Hebrews 11:1
How have you tested your faith?

KJV: Now faith is the substance of things hoped for, the evidence of things not seen.

NISV: Now faith is being sure of what we hope for and certain of what we do not see.

GNB: To have faith is to be sure of the things we hope for, to be certain of the things we cannot see.

TMB: The fundamental fact of existence is that this trust in God, this faith, is the firm foundation under everything that makes life worth living. It's our handle on what we can't see.

It is very hard to understand and accept the things we cannot see. But God says, "I will make these unseen things real to you if you trust in Me." We learn to trust Him more when we pray and read the Bible.

What is the most difficult concept about faith for you to comprehend?

march 8

Daniel 2:19a–21
Have you ever thought about the kings or monarchs that are still ruling many countries?

KJV: Then the secret was revealed unto Daniel in a night vision. Then Daniel blessed the God of Heaven. [20] Daniel answered and said, "Blessed be the name of God for ever and ever: for wisdom and might are his: [21] And he changeth the times and the seasons: he removeth kings, and setteth up kings: he giveth wisdom unto the wise, and knowledge to them that know understanding:"

NISV: …Then Daniel praised the God of heaven and said: [20] "Praise be to the name of God for ever and ever; wisdom and power are his, [21] He changes times and seasons; he sets up kings and deposes them. He gives wisdom to the wise and knowledge to the discerning."

GNB: Then the same night the mystery was revealed to Daniel in a vision, and he praised the God of heaven. [Daniel said:] [20] "God is wise and powerful! Praise him forever and ever. [21] He controls the times and the seasons; he makes and unmakes kings; it is he who gives wisdom and understanding."

TMB: That night the answer to the mystery was given to Daniel in a vision. Daniel blessed the God of heaven, saying,

> "Blessed be the name of God, forever and ever.
> He knows all, does all: He changes the seasons and guides history,
> He raises up kings and also brings them down,
> He provides both intelligence and discernment."

Daniel knew God would take care of him whether in a lowly prison or in a high position. Not only would God take care of him, God would also take care of King Nebuchadnezzar and all the kings to come after him. We need to understand that God is still taking care of all the nations and kings of the world today. May we have the confidence and peace of Daniel that God is everywhere.

How much are you like Daniel?

march 9

Job 33:31, 33
Job had a lot of problems and was listening to his "friends." But in the end, Job listened to God. Can we hold our peace, and can we be silent long enough to listen to God?

KJV: Mark well, O Job, hearken unto me: hold thy peace, and I will speak…[33]…Hold thy peace, and I shall teach thee wisdom.

NISV: "Pay attention, Job, and listen to me; be silent, and I will speak…[33]…be silent and I will teach you wisdom."

GNB: Now, Job, listen to what I am saying; Be quiet and let me speak…[33]…and I will teach you how to be wise.

TMB: "Keep listening, Job. Don't interrupt—I'm not finished yet…Meanwhile, keep listening. Don't distract me with interruptions. I'm going to teach you the basics of wisdom."

God is the only One that truly knows the outcome of our lives. Listen to Him, He is calling you.

Do we listen for the answer when we ask God a question?

march 10

Psalm 31:23-24
Is it hard for you to trust the Lord with everything?

KJV: O love the Lord, all ye his saints: for the Lord preserveth the faithful, and plentifully rewardeth the proud doer. 24 Be of good courage, and he shall strengthen your heart, all ye that hope in the Lord.

NISV: Love the Lord, all his saints! The Lord preserves the faithful, but the proud he pays back in full. 24 Be strong and take heart, all you who hope in the Lord.

GNB: Love the Lord, all his faithful people. The Lord protects the faithful, but punishes the proud as they deserve. 24 Be strong, be courageous, all you that hope in the Lord.

TMB: Love God, all you saints; God takes care of all who stay close to him, But he pays back in full those arrogant enough to go it alone. 24 Be brave. Be strong. Don't give up. Expect God to get here soon.

It is hard to turn everything over to God, but when you do, you will be amazed at the results.

What problem are you dealing with for which you can't find a answer? Did you ever consider asking for God's help?

march 11

Luke 6:38
Do you give to God and others joyfully?
Do you help those around you just
because they are there?

KJV: Give, and it shall be given unto you; good measure, pressed down, and shaken together, and running over, shall men give into your bosom. For with the same measure that ye mete withal it shall be measured to you again.

NISV: "Give, and it will be given to you. A good measure, pressed down, shaken together and running over, will be poured into your lap. For with the measure you use, it will be measured to you."

GNB: Give to others, and God will give to you. Indeed, you will receive a full measure, a generous helping, poured into your hands-all that you can hold. The measure you use for others is the one that God will use for you.

TMB: "Give away your life; you'll find life given back, but not merely given back—given back with bonus and blessing. Giving, not getting, is the way. Generosity begets generosity."

When you help others with a joyful heart, the satisfaction of a job well done is very fulfilling. Jesus is watching and will give you a heavenly reward far greater than you can ever imagine or receive on earth.

Have you helped anyone recently?

march 12

2 Corinthians 12:9
Do you ever ask the Lord to take care of a special problem? In verses 7 and 8 Paul is asking the Lord to take away his pain and a physical ailment. The Lord said to Paul:

KJV: ..."My grace is sufficient for thee: for my strength is made perfect in weakness." Most gladly therefore will I rather glory in my infirmities, that the power of Christ may rest upon me.

NISV: But he said to me, "My grace is sufficient for you, for my power is made perfect in weakness." Therefore I will boast all the more gladly about my weaknesses, so that Christ's power may rest on me.

GNB: But his answer was: "My grace is all you need, for my power is strongest when you are weak." I am most happy, then, to be proud of my weaknesses, in order to feel the protection of Christ's power over me.

TMB: My grace is enough; it's all you need. My strength comes into its own in your weakness.

Sometimes the Lord answers our prayers right away, sometimes He says maybe, sometimes He says wait. But the hardest answers to accept are when He says no. He knows the future and has other ideas and plans for us, we need to learn to trust Him and be happy where we are. Give into the strength, love, and grace that Christ has offered to us. His answer is the best and only answer.

If you have trouble thinking of prayers to pray, remember, God, just wants to know that you need Him. Just pray to Him like you would talk to a friend. If you want to start with a formal prayer, use this prayer and add whatever you need to say. Part of this prayer was suggested by Charles Stanley, on one of his weekly television programs:

"I now begin a blessed new day, to trust You, Jesus, everyway. I thank You for Your constant care and know that You are always there. Protect and cover our family with the blood of Jesus."

march 13

Romans 8:5-6
Do you "ride the fence" trying to be a Christian but running around with the other crowd?

KJV: For they that are after the flesh do mind the things of the flesh; but they that are after the Spirit the things of the Spirit. ⁶ For to be carnally minded *is* death; but to be spiritually minded *is* life and peace.

NISV: Those who live according to the sinful nature have their minds set on what that nature desires; but those who live in accordance with the Spirit have their minds set on what the Spirit desires. ⁶ The mind of sinful man is death, but the mind controlled by the Spirit is life and peace;

GNB: Those who live as their human nature tells them to, have their minds controlled by what human nature wants. Those who live as the Spirit tells them to, have their minds controlled by what the Spirit wants. ⁶ To be controlled by human nature results in death; to be controlled by the Spirit results in life and peace.

TMB: Those who think they can do it on their own end up obsessed with measuring their own moral muscle but never get around to exercising it in real life. ⁶ Those who trust God's action in them find that God's Spirit is in them—living and breathing God!

It is amazing how the Holy Spirit works in our lives. When we know we are not following God's will, we may think we are having a good time; but when the lights are out and we have no one to "have fun with," the peace we are longing for is hard to find. The old song "Take Your Burdens to the Lord" says, "If you trust and never doubt, He will surely bring you out. Take your burdens to the Lord and leave them there." Trusting Jesus is the only way to have peace in your heart. Ask Him to come into your heart and give you a new beginning.

Was it easy saying no to something you didn't agree with? How did you take a stand for what you believe?

march 14

Romans 8:35, 37
Do your friends try to make you doubt
your allegiance to Christ?

KJV: Who shall separate us from the love of Christ? *shall* tribulation, or distress, or persecution, or famine, or nakedness, or peril, or sword?…[37] Nay, in all these things we are more than conquerors through him that loved us.

NISV: Who shall separate us from the love of Christ? Shall trouble or hardship or persecution or famine or nakedness or danger or sword?…[37] No, in all these things we are more than conquerors through him who loved us.

GNB: Who, then, can separate us from the love of Christ? Can trouble do it, or hardship or persecution or hunger or poverty or danger or death?…[37] No, in all these things we have complete victory through him who loved us!

TMB: Do you think anyone is going to be able to drive a wedge between us and Christ's love for us? There is no way! Not trouble, not hard times, not hatred, not hunger, not homelessness, not bullying threats, not backstabbing, not even the worst sins listed in scripture…None of this fazes us because Jesus loves us.

No one can come between God and us. The song "We Are More Than Conquerors" says, "The Christ that dwells within us is the greatest power we know....He's the captain of our fate."

The people who try to persuade us to abandon God don't understand that God is taking care of us and we don't need them or their doctrine of hate, evil, or false religion. God is the creator of everything and rules everything. Ask them if they have peace in their soul. God will give them peace.

Make a list of those you see each day. Do you think they have peace? Can they tell you are at peace?

march 15

Proverbs 27:5
Have you ever tried to correct a wrong
with someone who is close to you?

KJV: Open rebuke is better than secret love.

NISV: Better is open rebuke than hidden love.

GNB: Better to correct someone openly than to let him think you don't care for him at all.

TMB: A spoken reprimand is better than approval that's never expressed.

If you love a person and you know what you need tell them will upset them, pray and ask the Lord to help you say the right thing. It is best they learn about the problem from someone they love and loves them. However, take someone along with you that is not involved with the situation or person. God will help you to say the right thing. Don't expect the person to thank you; they might be resentful. In time the person will come to realize how much you love them and how important it was that they be made aware of the problem.

Have you had to confront someone and found it very difficult to say something? What did you do?

march 16

Psalm 37:3-5
Where do you look to find happiness?

KJV: Trust in the Lord, and do good; so shalt thou dwell in the land, and verily thou shalt be fed. ⁴ Delight thyself also in the Lord; and he shall give thee the desires of thine heart. ⁵ Commit thy way unto the Lord; trust also in him; and he shall bring it to pass.

NISV: Trust in the Lord and do good; dwell in the land and enjoy safe pasture. ⁴ Delight yourself in the Lord and he will give you the desires of your heart. ⁵ Commit your way to the Lord; trust in him and he will do this.

GNB: Trust in the Lord and do good; live in the land and be safe. ⁴ Seek your happiness in the Lord, and he will give you your heart's desire. ⁵ Give yourself to the Lord; trust in him, and he will help you.

TMB: Get insurance with God and do a good deed, settle down and stick to your last. Keep company with God, get in on the best. Open up before God, keep nothing back; he'll do whatever needs to be done:

We can have a great deal of money, a big home, car, clothes, and lots of toys; but it will not give us real joy. The only real happiness and joy comes from within; by having the power of God on your side. He will give you the kind of peace that only the Lord can give.

What brings you happiness?

march 17

Galatians 2:16
What laws should we follow?

KJV: Knowing that a man is not justified by the works of the law, but by the faith of Jesus Christ, even we have believed in Jesus Christ, that we might be justified by the faith of Christ, and not by the works of the law: for by the works of the law shall no flesh be justified.

NISV: Know that a man is not justified by observing the law, but by faith in Jesus Christ. So we, too, have put our faith in Christ Jesus that we may be justified by faith in Christ and not by observing the law, no one will be justified.

GNB: Yet we know that a person is put right with God only through faith in Jesus Christ, never by doing what the Law requires. We, too, have believed in Christ Jesus in order to be put right with God through our faith in Christ, and not by doing what the Law requires. For no one is put right with God by doing what the Law requires.

TMB: We know very well that we are not set right with God by rule-keeping but only through personal faith in Jesus Christ. How do we know? We tried it—and we had the best system of rules the world has ever seen! Convinced that no human being can please God by self-improvement, we believed in Jesus as the Messiah so that we might be set right before God by trusting in the Messiah, not by trying to be good.

In these verses Paul is assuring the people in Antioch that Jesus died for their sins and they are covered by the grace of God. The old laws have been washed clean by the blood of Jesus. We are saved by the grace of Jesus and through our faith in Him.

march 18

John 6:28-35
Wouldn't it be great to never be hungry or thirsty again?

The day after the miracle of five loaves and two fishes, the people were looking for Jesus in Capernaum. When they found him...

KJV: 28 Then they said unto him, "What shall we do, that we might work the works of God? 29 *[Jesus said,]* "This is the work of God, that ye believe on him whom he hath sent...." 30 *[They asked what sign he would show them so they would believe.]* 31 Our fathers did eat manna in the desert..." 32 "Verily, verily, I say unto you, Moses gave you not that bread from heaven; but my Father giveth you the true bread from heaven. 33 For the bread of God is he which cometh down from heaven, and giveth life unto the world." 34 Then said they unto him, Lord, evermore give us this bread. 35 And Jesus said unto them, "I am the bread of life: he that cometh to me shall never hunger: and he that believeth on me shall never thirst."

NISV: 28 "What must we do to do the works God requires?" 29 "The work of God is this: "to believe in the one he has sent." 30 *[what signs will you give us...]* 31 "Our forefathers ate the manna in the desert; as it is written: He gave them bread from heaven to eat."

³² Jesus said to them, "I tell you the truth, it is not Moses who has given you the bread from heaven, but it is my Father who gives you the true bread from heaven. For the bread of God is he who comes down from heaven and gives life to the world." ³⁴ "Sir," they said, "from now on give us this bread." ³⁵ Then Jesus declared, "I am the bread of life. He who comes to me will never go hungry, and he who believes in me will never be thirsty."

GNB: ²⁸ So they asked him, "What can we do in order to do what God wants us to do? ²⁹ Jesus answered, "What God wants you to do is to believe in the one he sent. ³⁰…What miracle will you perform so we may see it and believe you? ³¹ Our ancestors ate manna in the desert…" ³² What Moses gave you was not the bread from heaven; it is my Father who gives you the real bread from heaven. ³³ For the bread that God gives is he who comes down from heaven and gives life to the world." ³⁴ "Sir," they asked him, "give us this bread always." ³⁵ "I am the bread of life," Jesus told them. "He who comes to me will never be hungry; he who believes in me will never be thirsty."

TMB: To that they said, "Well, what do we do then to get in on God's works?" Jesus said, "Throw your lot in with the One that God has sent. That kind of a commitment gets you in on God's works." They waffled: "Why don't you give us a clue about who you are, just a hint of what's going on? When we see what's up, we'll commit ourselves. Show us what you can do. Moses fed our ancestors with bread in the desert. It says so in the Scriptures: `He gave them bread from heaven to eat.'" Jesus responded, "The real significance of that Scripture is not that Moses gave you bread from heaven but that my Father is right now offering you bread from heaven, the *real* bread. The bread of God came down out of heaven and is giving life to the world." They jumped at that: "Master, give us this bread, now and forever!" Jesus said, "I am the Bread of Life. The person who aligns with me hungers no more and thirsts no more, ever."

The Lord can cure your spiritual hunger and thirst. John 4:14 says, "...But the water I shall give him shall be in him a well of water springing up into everlasting life" (KJV). Just trust in Him and He will fill you with His everlasting water, His spirit and peace.

march 19

Romans 12:14, 19-21
How should we treat our enemies?

KJV: [14] Bless them which persecute you: bless, and curse not...[19] "Vengeance is mine; I will repay," saith the LORD. [20] Therefore if thine enemy hunger, feed him; If he thirst, give him drink: for in so doing thou shalt heap coals of fire on his head. [21] Be not overcome of evil, but overcome evil with good.

NISV: [14] Bless those who persecute you; bless and do not curse...[19] It is mine to avenge; I will repay, says the LORD. [20] "If your enemy is hungry, feed him; if he is thirsty, give him something to drink. In doing this, you will heap burning coals on his head." [21] Do not be overcome by evil, but overcome evil with good.

GNB: [14] Ask God to bless those who persecute you—yes, ask him to bless, not to curse...[19] Never take revenge..."I will take revenge, I will pay back says the LORD." [20] "If your enemy is hungry, feed him: if he is thirsty, give him a drink; for by doing this you will make him burn with shame." [21] Do not let evil defeat you; instead, conquer evil with good.

TMB: Bless your enemies; no cursing under your breath.... Don't insist on getting even; that's not for you to do. "I'll do the judging, "says God." "I'll take care of it." Our Scriptures tell us that if you see your enemy hungry, go buy that person lunch, or if he's thirsty, get him a drink. Your generosity will surprise him with goodness. Don' let evil get the best of you; get the best of evil by doing good.

Jesus also says in Romans 12:15, "Rejoice with them that do rejoice, and weep with them that weep." Romans 12:18 says, "If it be possible, as much as lieth in you, live peaceably with all men" (KJV).

How do you treat those who you feel are persecuting you?

march 20

Luke 18:16-17
Will you come to Jesus in an innocent and childlike way?

The disciples were scolding the people because they were bothering Jesus with their children:

KJV: But Jesus called them unto him, and said, "Suffer little children to come unto me, and forbid them not: for of such is the kingdom of God. ¹⁷ Verily I say unto you, whosoever shall not receive the kingdom of God as a little child shall in no wise enter therein."

NISV: But Jesus called the children to him and said, "Let the little children come to me, and do not hinder them, for the kingdom of God belongs to such as these. ¹⁷ I tell you the truth, anyone who will not receive the kingdom of God like a little child will never enter it."

GNB: But Jesus called the children to him and said, "Let the children come to me and do not stop them, because the Kingdom of God belongs to such as these. ¹⁷ Remember this! Whoever does not receive the Kingdom of God like a child will never enter it."

TMB: Jesus called them back. "Let these children alone. Don't get between them and me. These children are the kingdom's pride and joy. Mark this: Unless you accept God's kingdom in the simplicity of a child, you'll never get in."

Our Father in heaven wants us to come to Him in a childlike way. He wants to teach us from the beginning of our spiritual relationship about His love and care for us. He will show us His strength and mercy. All we need to do is accept what He offers. Just ask Jesus to come into your heart. Allow God to teach and lead you as a Father would. If you have never had an attentive father, God will fill that emptiness and be available to you like a father.

What is the difference in the relationship with you and your earthly father and you and your heavenly Father?

march 21

1 Corinthians 8:6
Paul talks to his people about idols:
1 Corinthians 8:4 says, "an idol stands for something that does not really exist" (GNB).

KJV: "But to us *there is but* one God, the Father, of whom *are* all things, and we in him; and *one* LORD Jesus Christ, by whom *are* all things, and we by him."

NISV: "yet for us there is but one God, the Father, from whom all things came and for whom we live; and there is but one LORD, Jesus Christ, through whom all things came and through whom we live."

GNB: "Yet there is for us only one God, the Father, who is the Creator of all things and for whom we live; and there is only one LORD, Jesus Christ, through whom all things were created and through whom we live."

TMB: Some people say, quite rightly, that idols have no actual existence, that there's nothing to them, that there is no God other than our one God, that no matter how many of these so-called gods are named and worshiped they still don't add up to anything but a tall story. They say—again, quite rightly—that there is only one God the Father, that everything comes from him, and that he wants us to live for him. Also, they say that there is only one Master—Jesus the Messiah—and that everything is for his sake, including us. Yes. It's true.

God has blessed us with all the things He created. We need look only to Him to fill our lives. To be strong in the Lord, we should not worship anything other than the Lord Jesus Christ.

What is your greatest blessing?

march 22

Romans 5:12
Who is a sinner?

KJV: Wherefore, as by one man, sin entered into the world, and death by sin; and so death passed upon all men, for that all have sinned.

NISV: Therefore, just as sin entered the world through one man, and death through sin, and in this way death came to all men, because all sinned.

GNB: Sin came into the world through one man, and his sin brought death with it. As a result, death has spread to the whole human race because everyone has sinned.

TMB: *The Death-Dealing Sin, the Life-Giving Gift.* You know the story of how Adam landed us in the dilemma we're in—first sin, then death, and no one exempt from either sin or death. That sin disturbed relations with God in everything and everyone, but the extent of the disturbance was not clear until God spelled it out in detail to Moses.

We are all sinners saved by the grace of God. If we ask Jesus into our hearts, He will save us from our sins. When we accept Him, He will give us eternal life and fill us with His power.

Sign in to www.Godtube.org to learn more about coping with this sad world.

march 23

Colossians 3:16
What do you do with the wisdom and knowledge God has given to you?

KJV: Let the word of Christ dwell in you richly in all wisdom; teaching and admonishing one another in psalms and hymns and spiritual songs, singing with grace in your hearts to the LORD.

NISV: Let the word of Christ dwell in you richly as you teach and admonish one another with all wisdom, and as you sing psalms, hymns and spiritual songs with gratitude in your hearts to God.

GNB: Christ's message in all its richness must live in your hearts. Teach and instruct one another with all wisdom. Sing psalms, hymns, and sacred songs: sing to God with thanksgiving in your hearts.

TMB: Let the Word of Christ—the Message—have the run of the house. Give it plenty of room in your lives. Instruct and direct one another using good common sense. And sing, sing your hearts out to God!

We can sing our way through the day. The song "Singing, I Go" says: Singing, I go along life's road, Praising the Lord, praising the Lord; Singing, I go along life's road, For Jesus has lifted my load." Words by Eliza E. Hewitt and Music by William J. Kirkpatrick. *You will be joyful when the Lord puts a song in your heart.*

march 24

Psalm 138:8
What is the Lord's purpose for your life?

KJV: The LORD will perfect that which concerneth me: thy mercy, O LORD, endureth for ever: forsake not the works of thine own hands.

NISV: The LORD will fulfill his purpose for me; your love, O LORD, endures forever—do not abandon the works of your hands.

GNB: You will do everything you have promised; LORD, your love is eternal. Complete the work that you have begun.

TMB: Finish what you started in me God. Your love is eternal—don't quit on me now.

We can depend on the Lord to show us His intentions for us. To learn more in detail about what He has in store for you, read the Purpose Driven Life by Rick Warren, from Zondervan publishers.

march 25

John 7:16–17
Whose doctrine was Jesus teaching at the
Festival of Shelters? What do you believe?

KJV: Jesus answered them, and said, "My doctrine is not mine, but his that sent me. ¹⁷ If any man will do his will, he shall know of the doctrine, whether it be of God, or *whether* I speak of myself."

NISV: Jesus answered, "My teaching is not my own. It comes from him who sent me. ¹⁷ If anyone chooses to do God's will, he will find out whether my teaching comes from God or whether I speak on my own."

GNB: Jesus answered, "What I teach is not my own teaching, but it comes from God, who sent me. ¹⁷ Whoever is willing to do what God wants will know whether what I teach comes from God or whether I speak on my own authority."

TMB: Jesus said, "I didn't make this up. What I teach comes from the One who sent me. Anyone who wants to do his will can test this teaching and know whether it's from God or whether I'm making it up."

If people are questioning you about what you believe, these are great verses. Ask them if they have ever asked Jesus to come into their hearts and lives. You simply can't know or understand God without this commitment. Do they have peace in their heart because of what or whom they believe in or worship? Only God can give them peace that is beyond all human understanding.

march 26

Acts 3:6-8
Do we always get the answer we are expecting from God in our prayers? Will money answer all our problems and needs?

John and Peter were on their way to the "Beautiful Gate" at the Temple in Jerusalem. A man who had been lame all his life saw them and was begging for them to give him something—he wanted money.

KJV: Then Peter said, Silver and gold have I none; but such as I have give I thee: In the name of Jesus Christ of Nazareth rise up and walk. ⁷ And he took him by the right hand, and lifted him up and immediately his feet and ankle bones received strength. ⁸ And he leaping up stood, and walked, and entered with them into the temple walking and leaping and praising God.

NISV: Then Peter said, "Silver or gold I do not have, but what I have I give you. In the name of Jesus of Nazareth, walk." ⁷ Taking him by the right hand, he helped him up, and instantly the man's feet and ankles became strong. ⁸ He jumped to his feet and began to walk. Then he went with them into the temple courts, walking and jumping, and praising God.

GNB: But Peter said to him, "I have no money at all, but I give you what I have: in the name of Jesus Christ of Nazareth I order you to get up and walk!" ⁷ Then he took him by his right hand and helped him up. At once the man's feet and ankles became strong; ⁸ he jumped up, stood on his feet, and started walking around. Then he went into the Temple with them, walking and jumping and praising God.

TMB: Peter said, "I don't have a nickel to my name, but what I do have, I give you: In the name of Jesus Christ of Nazareth, walk!" He grabbed him by the right hand and pulled him up. In an instant his feet and ankles became firm. The man went into the temple with them, Walking back and forth, dancing and praising God.

The Lord does not always give us what we ask for, but He gives us what we need.

march 27

Acts 3:13, 15-16
Do you have enough faith to let the Lord heal you?

After a lame man was healed, he went into the Temple praising God. "The people were all surprised and were amazed at what had happened to him" (GNB).

KJV: *[Peter said to them]* The God of Abraham, and of Isaac, and of Jacob, the God of our fathers, hath glorified his Son Jesus; whom ye delivered up, and denied him in the presence of Pilate, when he was determined to let him go…[15] And killed the Prince of life, whom God hath raised from the dead: whereof we are witnesses. [16] And his name through faith in his name hath made this man strong, whom ye see and know: yea, the faith which is by him hath given him this perfect soundness in the presence of you all.

NISV: *[Peter said to them]* The God of Abraham, Isaac and Jacob, the God of our fathers, has glorified his servant Jesus. You handed him over to be killed, and you disowned him before, Pilate, though he had decided to let him go…[15] You killed the author of life, but God raised him from the dead. We are witnesses of this. [16] By faith in the name of Jesus, this man whom you see and know was made strong. It is Jesus' name and the faith that comes through him that has given this complete healing to him, as you can all see.

GNB: *[Peter said to them]* ¹³ The God of Abraham. Isaac, and Jacob, the God of our ancestors, has given divine glory to his Servant Jesus. But you handed him over to the authorities…¹⁵ You killed the one who leads to life, but God raised him from death—and we are witnesses to this. ¹⁶ It was the power of his name that gave strength to his lame man. What you see and know was done by faith in his name; it was faith in Jesus that has made him well as you can all see.

TMB: *[Peter said to them]* The God of Abraham and Isaac and Jacob, the God of our ancestors, has glorified his Son Jesus. The very One that Pilate called innocent, you repudiated. …You no sooner killed the Author of Life than God raised him from the dead—and we're the witnesses. Faith in Jesus' name put this man, whose condition you know so well, on his feet—yes, faith and nothing but faith put this man healed and whole right before your eyes.

The faith the Lord gives us will help us accept what He can do for us.

march 28

Ephesians 3:20-21
What is the most important thing you asked God to do for you?

KJV: Now unto him that is able to do exceeding abundantly above all that we ask or think, according to the power that worketh in us. ²¹ Unto him be glory in the church by Christ Jesus throughout all ages, world without end. Amen.

NISV: Now to him who is able to do immeasurably more than all we ask or imagine, according to his power that is at work within us, ²¹ to him be glory in the church and in Christ Jesus throughout all generations, for ever and ever! Amen.

GNB: To him who by means of his power working in us is able to do so much more than we can ever ask for, or even think of; ²¹ to God be the glory in the church and in Christ Jesus for all time, for ever and ever! Amen.

TMB: God can do anything, you know—far more than you could ever imagine or guess or request in your wildest dreams! He does it not by pushing us around but by working within us, his Spirit deeply and gently within us.

    Glory to God in the church!
    Glory to God in the Messiah, in Jesus!
    Glory down all the generations!

Glory through all millennia! Oh, yes!

We limit the power of God because we lack faith and trust. What can you do to increase God's power in your life?

march 29

Ephesians 4:17-18
"The New Life in Christ"

kjv: This I say therefore, and testify in the Lord, that ye henceforth walk not as other Gentiles walk, in the vanity of their mind. [18] Having the understanding darkened, being alienated from the life of God through the ignorance that is in them, because of the blindness of their heart.

nisv: So I tell you this, and insist on it in the Lord, that you must no longer live as the Gentiles do, in the futility of their thinking. [18] They are darkened in their understanding and separated from the life of God because of the ignorance that is in them due to the hardening of their hearts.

gnb: In the Lord's name, then, I warn you: do not continue to live like the heathen whose thoughts are worthless. [18] and whose minds are in the dark. They have no part in the life that God gives, for they are completely ignorant and stubborn.

tmb: And so I insist—and God backs me up on this—that there be no going along with the crowd, the empty-headed, mindless crowd. They've refused for so long to deal with God that they've lost touch not only with God but with reality itself. They can't think straight anymore.

Until we accept Christ as our Savior, we are as heathen to God in heaven. The Lord through His scripture teaches us how to live and be a witness for Him.

How does the Lord want us to live our lives in front of others?

march 30

Romans 6:5-6
Have you been baptized?

Paul talks to the church about being baptized. [When we were baptized into His death we were buried with Him and shared His death through baptism] Romans 6:4…"just as Christ was raised from the dead through the glory of the Father, we too may live a new life" (NISV).

KJV: For we have been planted together in the likeness of his death, we shall be also in the likeness of his resurrection: ⁶ Knowing this, that our old man is crucified with him, that the body of sin might be destroyed, that henceforth we should not serve sin.

NISV: If we have been united with him like this in his death, we will certainly also be united with him in his resurrection. ⁶ For we know that our old self was crucified with him so that the body of sin might be done away with, that we should no longer be slaves to sin—

GNB: For since we have become one with him in dying as he did, in the same way we shall be one with him by being raised to life as he was. ⁶ And we know that our old being has been put to death with Christ on his cross, in order that the power of the sinful self might be destroyed, so that we should no longer be the slaves of sin.

TMB: That's what baptism into the life of Jesus means.

When we are lowered into the water, it is like the burial of Jesus; when we are raised up out of the water, it is like the resurrection of Jesus. Each of us is raised into a light-filled world by our Father so that we can see where we're going in our new grace-sovereign country.

The song "I Am the Resurrection" *tells us that:* "I am the resurrection and the life, He that believeth in me tho' He were dead, Yet shall He live,...And whosoever liveth and believeth in me shall never, never die." Words and music by Norman J. Clayton from John 11:25–26 (KJV).

The resurrection of Jesus has given us eternal life. God is our hope.
　　See March 31st for more details.

march 31

Romans 6:7-8
Have you received eternal life?

Through the resurrection of Jesus we have received eternal life.

- KJV: For he that is dead is freed from sin. ⁸ Now if we be dead with Christ, we believe that we shall also live with him.

- NISV: …Because anyone who has died has been freed from sin. ⁸ Now if we died with Christ, we believe that we will also live with him.

- GNB: For when a person dies, he is set free from the power of sin. ⁸ Since we have died with Christ, we believe that we will also live with him.

- TMB: Could it be any clearer? Our old way of life was nailed to the cross with Christ, a decisive end to that sin-miserable life—no longer at sin's every beck and call! What we believe is this: If we get included in Christ's sin-conquering death, we also get included in his life-saving resurrection.

In Romans 6:12-14 Sin must no longer rule our mortal bodies. ¹³…Instead, give yourselves to God, as those who have been brought from death to life, and surrender your whole being to him…¹⁴ Sin must not be your master: for you do not live under law but under God's grace. (GNB)

Have you decided the best alternative for your life?

april 1

Acts 15:11
Can you imagine how hard it would have been to follow all the old Jewish laws and customs?

Paul was in Jerusalem talking to the apostles and the elders about whether the Gentiles should be circumcised and be given the rules and laws of the Old Testament. Paul told them circumcision and the rules were from the law. The Gentiles were not under the law but under the cross and grace.

- KJV: *[Paul said,]* "But we believe that through the grace of the LORD Jesus Christ we shall be saved, even as they."
- NISV: *[Paul said,]* "No! We believe it is through the grace of our LORD Jesus that we are saved, just as they are."
- GNB: *[Paul said,]* "No! We believe and are saved by the grace of the LORD Jesus, just as they are."
- TMB: *[Paul said,]* "So why are you now trying to out-god God, loading these new believers down with rules that crushed our ancestors and crushed us, too? Don't we believe that we are saved because the Master Jesus amazingly and out of sheer generosity moved to save us just as he did those from beyond our nation: So what are we arguing about?"

We can thank God that we don't have to follow the letter of the Jewish law and He has saved us by His grace.

Have you ever experienced God's grace? What did God do for you?

april 2

Jude 1:24-25
How can we save ourselves from evil?

KJV: Now unto him that is able to keep you from falling, and to present you faultless before the presence of his glory with exceeding joy. ²⁵ To the only wise God our Saviour, be glory and majesty, dominion and power, both now and ever. Amen.

NISV: To him who is able to keep you from falling and to present you before his glorious presence without fault and with great joy—²⁵ to the only God our Savior be glory, majesty, power and authority, through Jesus Christ our Lord, before all ages, now and forevermore! Amen.

GNB: To him who is able to keep you from falling and to bring you faultless and joyful before his glorious presence—²⁵ to the only God our Savior, through Jesus Christ our Lord, be glory, majesty, might and authority, from all ages past, and now, and forever and ever! Amen.

TMB: And now to him who can keep you on your feet, standing tall in his bright presence, fresh and celebrating—to our one God, our only Savior, through Jesus Christ, our Master, be glory, majesty, strength, and rule before all time, and now, and to the end of all time. Yes.

God is the only one who can save us. The Lord intercedes for us and gives us a way to be precious in His sight. We need to give God all the glory and thanks for sending us His son.

Do you ever count your blessings?

april 3

1 Thessalonians 4:13–14
How can we know that we will be with Christ at His returning?

Paul is teaching the Macedonians about the Lord's second coming—as described in the book of Revelation.

KJV: But I would not have you to be ignorant, brethren, concerning them which are asleep, that ye sorrow not, even as others which have no hope. [14] For if we believe that Jesus died and rose again, even so them also which sleep in Jesus will God bring with him.

NISV: Brothers, we do not want you to be ignorant about those who fall asleep, or to grieve like the rest of men, who have no hope. [14] We believe that Jesus died and rose again and so we believe that God will bring with Jesus those who have fallen asleep in him.

GNB: Our brothers, we want you to know the truth about those who have died, so that you will not be sad, as are those who have no hope, [14] We believe that Jesus died and rose again, and so we believe that God will take back with Jesus those who have died believing in him.

TMB: And regarding the question, friends, that has come up about what happens to those already dead and buried, we don't want you in the dark any longer.

First off, you must not carry on over them like people who have nothing to look forward to, as if the grave were the last word. Since Jesus died and broke loose from the grave, God will most certainly bring back to life those who died in Jesus.

When we die we can know that our life has just begun. Are you ready?

For details go online and check out: www.lifesgreatestquestion.com/way_home.html

april 4

1 Thessalonians 4:15-16
Have you read about the signs of the second-coming of Jesus? Some people think it could happen in our lifetime.

In these verses Paul is teaching more about the second coming of Christ, as described in the book of Revelation.

KJV: For this we say unto you by the word of the Lord, that we which are alive and remain unto the coming of the Lord shall not prevent them which are asleep. [16] For the Lord himself shall descend from heaven with a shout, with the voice of the archangel, and with the trump of God: and the dead in Christ shall rise first.

NISV: According to the Lord's own word, we tell you that we who are still alive, who are left till the coming of the Lord, will certainly not precede those who have fallen asleep. [16] For the Lord himself will come down from heaven, with a loud command, with the voice of the archangel and with the trumpet call of God, and the dead in Christ will rise first.

GNB: What we are teaching you now is the Lord's teaching:…we who are alive on the day the Lord comes will not go ahead of those who have died. [16] There will be the shout of command, the archangel's voice, the sound of God's trumpet, and the Lord himself will come down from heaven. Those who have died believing in Christ will rise to life first.

TMB: And then this: We can tell you with complete confidence—we have the Master's word on it—that when the Master comes again to get us, those of us who are still alive will not get a jump on the dead and leave them behind. In actual fact, they'll be ahead of us. The Master himself will give the command. Archangel thunder! God's trumpet blast! He'll come down from heaven and the dead in Christ will rise—they'll go first.

What a glorious day when we see Jesus and are taken up to live with Him.

april 5

1 Thessalonians 4:17-18
What will happen to the believers that are alive when Christ comes to earth again?

KJV: Then we which are alive *and* remain shall be caught up together with them in the clouds to meet the Lord in the air. And so shall we ever be with the Lord. ¹⁸ Wherefore comfort one another with these words.

NISV: After that, *[the people who have fallen asleep have been taken to heaven]* we who are still alive and are left will be caught up together with them in the clouds to meet the Lord in the air. And so we will be with the Lord forever. ¹⁸ Therefore encourage each other with these words.

GNB: then we who are living at that time will be gathered up along with them in the clouds to meet the Lord in the air. And so we will always be with the Lord. ¹⁸ So then, encourage one another with these words.

TMB: Then the rest of us who are still alive at the time will be caught up with them into the clouds to meet the Master. Oh, we'll be walking on air! And then there will be one huge family reunion with the Master. So reassure one another with these words.

An old hymn "Oh, That Will Be Glory" *talks about when we see Jesus. The words are…* When all my labors and trials are o'er And I am safe on that beautiful shore, Just to be near the dear Lord I adore Will through the ages be glory for me. Glory for Me…When by His grace I shall look on His face, That will be glory, be glory for me. Words and music by Charles H. Gabriel .

Will we know when the Lord is coming back? See 1 Thessalonians 5:2 (KJV) (April 6th).
   What are your thoughts about the second coming of Jesus?

april 6

1 Thessalonians 5:2
What have you done to prepare for Jesus returning to the earth?

KJV: For yourselves know perfectly that the day of the Lord so cometh as a thief in the night.

NISV: for you know very well that the day of the Lord will come like a thief in the night.

GNB: For you yourselves know very well that the Day of the Lord will come as a thief comes at night.

TMB: You know as well as I that the day of the Master's coming can't be posted on our calendars. He won't call ahead and make an appointment any more than a burglar would.

No one knows when the Lord is coming back! The most important thing we can know is that we are prepared to meet Him whenever He comes. Are you ready? Ask Him to come into your life to forgive your sins and give you eternal life. All He needs is for you to ask Him, accept His word, and trust in Him. He wants to be your companion and guide.

april 7

Psalm 6:2
When do you call on the Lord?

KJV: Have mercy upon me, O LORD; for I *am* weak: O LORD, heal me; for my bones are vexed.

NISV: Be merciful to me, LORD, for I am faint; O LORD, heal me, for my bones are in agony.

GNB: I am worn out, O LORD; have pity on me! Give me strength; I am completely exhausted and my whole being is deeply troubled.

TMB: Treat me nice for a change; I'm so starved for affection.

When things are good, we seem to forget the Lord. But when things get bad, we can't find Him fast enough. He wants to hear from us in good and bad situations. Pray all the time. He will keep your life on track.

How are things going today? Do you need some help? Reread the above scripture! Ask the Lord to help you.

april 8

Psalm 6:3
We cry out to him—he says wait!

KJV: My soul is also sore vexed: but thou, O Lord, how long?

NISV: My soul is in anguish. How long, O Lord, how long?

GNB: How long, O Lord, will you wait to help me?

TMB: Can't you see I'm black and blue, beat up badly in bones and soul?

When will His help come? He will answer us when His time is right.

april 9

Psalm 24:1
To whom do the people of the earth belong?

KJV: The earth *is* the Lord's and the fullness thereof; the world, and they that dwell therein.

NISV: The earth is the Lord's and everything in it, the world, and all who live in it.

GNB: The world and all that is in it belong to the Lord; the earth and all who live on it are his.

TMB: God claims Earth and everything in it. God claims World and all who live on it.

The Lord made us and everything in and on the earth. Blessed be the name of the Lord.
   What do you find to be God's most wondrous work?

april 10

Psalm 25:4-5
Do you know the plans God has for you today?

KJV: Shew me they ways, O Lord teach me thy paths. ⁵ Lead me in thy truth; and teach me: for thou *art* the God of my salvation; on thee do I wait all the day.

NISV: Show me your ways, O Lord, teach me your paths; ⁵ guide me in your truth and teach me, for you are God my Savior, and my hope is in you all day long.

GNB: Teach me your ways, O Lord; make them known to me. ⁵ Teach me to live according to your truth, for you are my God, who saves me. I always trust in you.

TMB: Show me how you work, God; School me in your ways. ⁵ Take me by the hand; Lead me down the path of truth. You are my Savior, aren't you?

Ask the Lord to help you understand His plans. He tells the truth! How can we the doubt the Lord when He has given His life for us?

april 11

Isaiah 43:1–2
If the Lord will save Israel, how can we not trust Him to save us? We are His children who worship Him and trust Him for our saving grace.

KJV: But now saith the Lord that created thee, O Jacob, and he that formed thee, O Israel, Fear not: for I have redeemed thee, I have called thee by thy name; thou art mine. ² When thou passeth through the waters I *will be* with *thee:* and through the rivers, they shall not overflow thee: when thou walkest through the fire, though shall not be burned neither shall the flame kindle upon thee.

NISV: But now, this is what the Lord says—he who created you, O Jacob he who formed you, O Israel: Fear not, for I have redeemed you; I have summoned you by name; you are mine. ² When you pass through the waters, I will be with you; and when you pass through the rivers, they will not sweep over you. When you walk through the fire, you will not be burned; the flames will not set you ablaze.

GNB: Israel, the Lord who created you says. "Do not be afraid- I will save you. I have called you by name- you are mine. ² When you pass through deep waters, I will be with you; your troubles will not overwhelm you. When you pass through fire, you will not be burned; the hard trials that come will not hurt you.

TMB: But now, God's Message, the God who made you in the first place, Jacob, the One who got you started, Israel: "Don't be afraid, I've redeemed you. I've called your name. You're mine. When you're in over your head, I'll be there with you. When you're in rough waters, you will not go down. When you're between a rock and a hard place, it won't be a dead end—"

The Lord waits for Israel to find Him again. He has great patience and will never leave us. He will always give us answers, but they may not be what you expect. God is with us. We can depend on Him to do what He says He will do.

When you call on the Lord, do you expect to get the answers you want? Are you open to His answer?

april 12

Isaiah 43:3-4
What will God give in exchange for Israel's return?

The Lord continues to talk to the people of Israel.

KJV: For I *am* the LORD thy God, the Holy One of Israel, thy Saviour: I gave Egypt *for* the ransom, Ethiopia and Seba for thee ⁴ Since thou wast precious in my sight, thou hast been honorable and I have loved thee: therefore will I give men for thee, and people for thy life.

NISV: For I am the LORD, your God, the Holy One of Israel, your Savior.; I give Egypt for your ransom, Cush and Seba in your stead. ⁴ Since you are precious and honored in my sight, and because I love you, I will give men in exchange for you, and people in exchange for your life.

GNB: For I am the LORD your God, the holy God of Israel, who saves you. I will give up Egypt to set you free; I will give up Sudan and Seba. ⁴ I will give up whole nations to save your life, because you are precious to me and because I love you and give you honor.

TMB: Because I am God, your personal God, The Holy [God] of Israel, your Savior. I paid a huge price for you: all of Egypt, with rich Cush and Seba thrown in! *That's* how much you mean to me! *That's* how much I love you! I'd sell off the whole world to get you back, trade the creation just for you.

God said He would give up everything for the children of Israel to come back to Him. Then He gave His son for us because He knew we could never live up to all His laws. How much He loves us all.!

april 13

Isaiah 43:5
Where are all the people from the Jewish nation of Israel now?

KJV: Fear not: for I *am* with thee: I will bring thy seed from the east, and gather thee from the west;

NISV: Do not be afraid, for I am with you; I will bring your children from the east and gather you from the west.

GNB: Do not be afraid—I am with you! From the distant east and the farthest west I will bring your people home.

TMB: So don't be afraid: I'm with you. I'll round up all your scattered children, pull them in from east and west...

We are seeing many frightening things in the Middle East these days. The Lord loves Israel and is waiting for His people to come back to Him. Will we see the second coming of the Lord in our time? Lord, please come back to earth soon and take us to live in the place You have prepared for us.

april 14

Isaiah 43:6-7
Have you seen signs of the Jewish people returning to Israel?

KJV: I will say to the north, give them up; and to the south, keep not back: bring my sons from far, and my daughters from the ends of the earth; ⁷ Even every one that is called by my name: for I have created him for my glory, I have formed him; yea, I have made him.

NISV: I will say to the north, give them up! And to the south, Do not hold them back. Bring my sons from afar and my daughters from the ends of the earth—⁷ everyone who is called by my name, whom I created for my glory, whom I formed and made."

GNB: I will tell the north to let them go and the south not to hold them back. Let my people return from distant lands from every part of the world. ⁷ They are my own people, and I created them to bring me glory.

TMB: I'll send orders north and south "Send them back. Return my sons from distant lands, my daughters from faraway places. I want them back, every last one who bears my name, every man, woman, and child whom I created for my glory, yes, personally formed and made each one."

God's chosen people will be gathered together from everywhere to Israel. We are seeing many things happening in Israel.

David Dolan has lived in Israel and has studied the people and the country. His book is very informative about the situation. Read "Israel in Crisis" by David Dolan, published by Fleming H. Revell.

april 15

Proverbs 9:12
How do we find wisdom for our lives?

KJV: If thou be wise, thou shalt be wise for thyself: but *if* thou scornest, thou alone shall bear it.

NISV: If you are wise, your wisdom will reward you; if you are a mocker, you alone will suffer.

GNB: You are the one who will profit if you have wisdom, and if you reject it, you are the one who will suffer.

TMB: Live wisely and wisdom will permeate your life, mock life and life will mock you.

Look to the Lord for wisdom. The Lord rewards your use of His wisdom, but don't think you are wise without His help. To learn His wisdom, study the Bible; begin with Proverbs.

What is your favorite Proverb?

april 16

Proverbs 12:4
How should we treat our husbands?

KJV: A virtuous woman is a crown to her husband: but she that maketh ashamed is as rottenness in his bones.

NISV: A wife of noble character is her husband's crown, but a disgraceful wife is like decay in his bones.

GNB: A good wife is her husband's pride and joy; but a wife who brings shame on her husband is like a cancer in his bones.

TMB: A hearty wife invigorates her husband, but a frigid woman is cancer in the bones.

The Lord cherishes a woman who loves and takes care of her husband.
If you are married how do you treat your husband?

april 17

Proverbs 12:5
Who is our council? How do we find
those who are deceitful?

KJV: The thoughts of the righteous *are* right: *but* the counsels of the wicked *are* deceit.

NISV: The plans of the righteous are just, but the advice of the wicked is deceitful.

GNB: Honest people will treat you fairly; the wicked only want to deceive you.

TMB: The thinking of principled people makes for justice; the plots of degenerates corrupt.

The Lord wants us to be fair to all people. We need to live by God's principles not those of deceit, greed, and hate.

april 18

Proverbs 12:6
Does evil win when it is deceiving people?

KJV: The words of the wicked *are* to lie in wait for blood: but the mouth of the upright shall deliver them

NISV: The words of the wicked lie in wait for blood, but the speech of the upright rescues them.

GNB: The words of wicked men are murderous, but the words of the righteous rescue those who are threatened.

TMB: The words of the wicked kill; the speech of the upright saves.

Those who speak the truth will win. God will reward us for sticking up for what is right.

april 19

Proverbs 12:7
Can evil people prevail when God takes over?

KJV: The wicked are overthrown, and *are* not; but the house of the righteous shall stand.

NISV: Wicked men are overthrown and are no more, but the house of the righteous stands firm.

GNB: Wicked men meet their downfall and leave no descendants, but the families of righteous men live on.

TMB: Wicked people fall to pieces—there's nothing to them; the homes of good people hold together.

Disobey the Lord and you will perish. Serve the Lord and He will take care of you.

We can take the words of this song with us each day. The title of the song is "Under His Wings" *it says* Under His wings I am safely abiding, Tho the night deepens and tempests are wild; Still I can trust Him—I know He will keep me, He has redeemed me and I am His child. Under His wings,…Who from His love can sever? Under His wings my soul shall abide, Safely abide forever. Words by William O. Cushing and music by Ira D. Sankey.

april 20

Psalm 1:1
Will the Lord take care of us if we walk in the paths of evil?

Songs and prayers from Psalms. See April 23 for Psalm 1 from The Message Bible.

- KJV: Blessed *is* the man that walketh not in the council of the ungodly, nor standeth in the way of sinners, nor sitteth in the seat of the scornful.
- NISV: Blessed is the man who does not walk in the counsel of the wicked or stand in the way of sinners or sit in the seat of mockers.
- GNB: Happy are those who reject the advice of evil men, who do not follow the example of sinners or join those who have no use for God.
- TMB: How well God must like you—you don't hang out at Sin Saloon, you don't slink along Dead-End Road, you don't go to Smart-Mouth College.

God will bless His children as they follow Him.

april 21

Psalm 1:2-3
How well do you know the Bible?

Advice on how to live for God, from Psalms.

KJV: But his delight is in the law of the LORD; and in his law doth he meditate day and night. ³ And he shall be like a tree planted by the rivers of water, that bringeth forth his fruit in his season; his leaf also shall not wither; and whatsoever he doeth shall prosper.

NISV: But his delight is in the law of the LORD, and on his law he meditates day and night ³ He is like a tree planted by streams of water, which yields its fruit in season and whose leaf does not wither. Whatever he does prospers.

GNB: Happy are the people obeying God. …Instead, they find joy in obeying the Law of the LORD, and they study it day and night. ³ They are like tees that grow beside a stream, that bear fruit at the right time, and whose leaves do not dry up. They succeed in everything they do.

TMB: Instead you thrill to God's Word, you chew on Scripture day and night. You're a tree replanted in Eden, bearing fresh fruit every month. Never dropping a leaf, always in blossom.

If you teach Sunday school, challenge your students to memorize scriptures from the Bible. We need to have scriptures in our mind so they will be available to us when we don't have a Bible. Meditating on God's word each day will help our roots grow deep in Him and hold fast.

Do you have a favorite Bible verse? When was the last time you memorized a scripture verse?

april 22

Psalm 1:4-5
What happens to people that do not follow God?

KJV: The ungodly *are* not so but *are* like the chaff which the wind driveth away. ⁵ Therefore the ungodly shall not stand in the judgment, nor sinners in the congregation of the righteous.

NISV: Not so the wicked! They are like chaff that the wind blows away. ⁵ Therefore the wicked will not stand in the judgment, nor sinners in the assembly of the righteous.

GNB: But evil men are not like [those that follow God] this at all; they are like straw that the wind blows away. ⁵ Sinners will be condemned by God and kept apart from God's own people.

TMB: You're not at all like the wicked, who are mere windblown dust—Without defense in court, unfit company for innocent people.

God wants us to depend on Him and be dependable, and we must learn to trust Him with our lives.

april 23

Psalm 1:6
Why should we follow God?

KJV: For the LORD knoweth the way of the righteous: but the way of the ungodly shall perish.

NISV: For the LORD watches over the way of the righteous, but the way of the wicked will perish.

GNB: The righteous are guided and protected by the LORD, but the evil are on the way to their doom.

TMB: God charts the road you take. The road *they* take is Skid Row.

Psalm 1 from TMB:

"How well God must like you—you don't hang out at Sin Saloon, you don't slink along Dead-End Road, you don't go to Smart-Mouth College. Instead you thrill to God's Word, you chew on Scripture day and night. You're a tree replanted in Eden, bearing fresh fruit every month. Never dropping a leaf, always in blossom. You're not at all like the wicked, who are mere windblown dust—Without defense in court, unfit company for innocent people. God charts the road you take. The road *they* take is Skid Row."

Thank You, Lord, for allowing us to love and serve You. Thank You for watching over us.

april 24

1 Thessalonians 5:3
Should we pray for peace?

KJV: For when they shall say, Peace and safety: then sudden destruction cometh upon them, as travail upon a woman with child; and they shall not escape.

NISV: While people are saying, "Peace and safety," destruction will come on them suddenly, as labor pains on a pregnant woman, and they will not escape.

GNB: When people say, "Everything is quite and safe," then suddenly destruction will hit them! It will come suddenly as the pains that come upon a woman in labor, and people will not escape.

TMB: About the time everybody's walking around complacently, congratulating each other—"We've sure got it made! Now we can take it easy!"—suddenly everything will fall apart. It's going to come as suddenly and inescapably as birth pangs to a pregnant woman.

Do you think the entire world will ever see complete peace before Jesus comes back to earth? God does not promise us peace upon this earth at this time. God's Son is the only one that can bring peace to this world and that will happen when He returns to the earth. Praying for God's will in God's time will give us inner peace.

april 25

Psalm 2:2-3
"God's Chosen King" (GNB)

KJV: The kings of the earth set themselves, and the rulers take counsel together, against the LORD, and against his anointed, *saying*. ³ Let us break their bands asunder, and cast away their cords from us.

NISV: The kings of the earth take their stand and the rulers gather together against the LORD and against his Anointed One. ³ "Let us break their chains," they say, "and throw off their fetters."

GNB: Their kings revolt, their rulers plot together against the LORD and against the king he chose. ³ "Let us free ourselves from their rule," they say; "let us know of their control."

TMB: Earth-leaders push for position, Demagogues and delegates meet for summit talks, The God-deniers, the Messiah-defiers: ³ Let's get free of God! Cast loose from Messiah!

What a sad end will come to those rulers who deny God. Let us pray for leaders of our world that they may seek God's will.

Did you vote in the last election? What can we do to help our country?

april 26

Psalm 2:11
How should we serve the Lord? (GNB)

- KJV: Serve the LORD with fear, and rejoice with trembling.
- NISV: Serve the LORD with fear and rejoice with trembling
- GNB: Serve the LORD with fear: tremble and bow down to him.
- TMB: Worship God in adoring embrace, celebrate in trembling awe.

We should serve the Lord as our King. As in "Joy to the World" the song says, "Joy to the world the Lord has come, let earth receive their king. Let every heart prepare Him room and heaven and nature sing.…He rules the world with truth and grace." We are on earth to celebrate the God who made us. Words from Psalm 98 newly written by Isaac Watts and music by George F. Handel.

april 27

Psalm 4:1
"Evening Prayer for Help" (GNB)

KJV: Hear me when I call, O God of my righteousness: thou hast enlarged me *when I was* in distress;

NISV: Answer me when I call to you, O my righteous God. Give me relief from my distress; be merciful to me and hear my prayer.

GNB: Answer me when I pray, O God, my defender! When I was in trouble, you helped me. Be kind to me now and hear my prayer.

TMB: When I call, give me answers. God, take my side! Once, in a tight place, you gave me room. Now I'm in trouble again: grace me! hear me!

The Lord taught David great patience. David knew and trusted the Lord to answer. Dear Lord, please give us faith like David's.

april 28

Psalm 4:6-7
"Evening Prayer for Help" (GNB)

KJV: *There be* many that say, who will shew us *any* good?" LORD, lift thou up the light of thy countenance upon us. ⁷ Thou hast put gladness in my heart, more than in the time *that* their corn and their wine increased.

NISV: Many are asking, "Who can show us any good?" Let the light of your face shine upon us, O LORD. ⁷ You have filled my heart with greater joy than when their grain and new wine abound.

GNB: There are many who pray; "Give us more blessings, O LORD. Look on us with kindness!" ⁷ But the joy that you have given me is more than they will ever have with all their grain and wine.

TMB: Why is everyone hungry for *more?* "More, more," they say, "More, More." I have God's more-than-enough, More joy in one ordinary day

Real joy comes from inner peace that only the Lord can give. We only have to pray and trust God to lead us.

april 29

Psalm 4:8
Do you allow the Lord to give you peace?

KJV: I will both lay me down in peace, and sleep: for thou, LORD, only makest me dwell in safety.

NISV: I will lie down and sleep in peace, for you alone, O LORD, make me dwell in safety.

GNB: When I lie down, I go to sleep in peace; you alone, O LORD, keep me perfectly safe.

TMB: …At day's end I'm ready for sound sleep. For you, God, have put my life back together.

Have you found a special prayer that helps you?

What do you do to find peace? If we trust God, He will give us peace. Memorize a favorite scripture and say it when you are feeling alone. It will help you to get through your day. Let's trust God to give us peace. Memorize one of the verses above or part of John 14:27, "Peace I leave with you; my peace I give you. I do not give to you as the world gives. Do not let your heart be troubled and do not be afraid" (NISV).

april 30

Psalm 5:2–3
"A Prayer for Protection" (GNB)

KJV: Hearken unto the voice of my cry, my King, and my God: for unto thee will I pray: ³ My voice shalt thou hear in the morning, O LORD; in the morning will I direct *my* prayer unto thee, and will look up.

NISV: Listen to my cry for help, my King and my God, for to you I pray. ³ In the morning, O LORD, you hear my voice; in the morning I lay my requests before you and wait in expectation.

GNB: Listen to my cry for help, my God and King! I pray to you, O LORD ³ you hear my voice in the morning; at sunrise I offer my prayer and wait for your answer.

TMB: Every morning you'll hear me at it again. ³ Every morning I lay out the pieces of my life on your alter and watch for fire to descend.

We can trust the Lord to defend us against our enemies.

may 1

Psalm 6:4
"A Prayer for Help in Time of Trouble" (GNB)

KJV: Return O LORD, deliver my soul: oh save me for thy mercies' sake.

NISV: Turn, O LORD, and deliver me; save me because of your unfailing love.

GNB: Come and save me, LORD; in your mercy rescue me from death.

TMB: God, how long will it take for you to let up?

How is your patience? Sometimes it seems we are on our own, but God is there and will answer us in His time and protect us.

may 2

Psalm 6:8–9
God will hear our earnest prayers.

KJV: Depart from me, all ye workers of iniquity; for the LORD hath heard the voice of my weeping. ⁹ The LORD hath heard my supplication; the LORD will receive my prayer.

NISV: Away from me, all you who do evil, for the LORD has heard my weeping, ⁹ The LORD accepts my prayer.

GNB: Keep away from me, you evil men! The LORD hears my weeping; ⁹ he listens to my cry for help and will answer my prayer.

TMB: Get out of here, you Devil's crew: at last God has heard my sobs. ⁹ My requests have all been granted, my prayers are answered.

The Lord teaches us patience. Lord, give us the patience to wait for Your answers.

may 3

Psalm 7:1
"A Prayer for Justice" (GNB)

KJV: O Lord my God, in thee do I put my trust: save me from all them that persecute me, and deliver me:

NISV: O Lord my God, I take refuge in you; save and deliver me from all who pursue me.

GNB: O Lord, my God, I come to you for protection; rescue me and save me from all who pursue me.

TMB: God! God! I am running to you for dear life, the chase is wild.

Do you feel persecuted? Place your trust in God. God will keep you safe from your enemies.

Treat your enemies with love. They won't know how to react Your enemy could become your best friend.

may 4

Psalm 8:3-4
"God's Glory and Man's Dignity" (GNB)

KJV: When I consider thy heavens, the work of thy fingers, the moon and the stars, which thou hast ordained; ⁴ What is man, that thou art mindful of him? and the son of man, that thou visitest him?

NISV: When I consider your heavens, the work of your fingers, the moon and the stars, which you have set in place, ⁴ what is man that you are mindful of him, the son of man that you care for him?

GNB: When I look at the sky, which you have made, at the moon and the stars, which you set in their places—⁴ what is man, that you think of him; mere man, that you care for him?

TMB: I look up at your macro-skies, dark and enormous, your handmade sky-jewelry, Moon and stars mounted in their settings. ⁴ Then I look at my micro-self and wonder, Why do you bother with us?

Thank you, Lord, for giving us such an amazing universe in which to live. We are in awe of the creation around us. Help us to enjoy all that You have provided for us. Thank You, Lord, for giving us Your grace so we may worship You.

There is a wonderful Creation Museum in Kentucky.

Adults and children will enjoy the many exhibits starting from the beginning of creation until the present time. It is open during the week and on Saturday. You can find it in Petersburg, Kentucky. It is about twenty miles east of the Cincinnati, Ohio, airport. Their website is www.creationmuseum.com.

What do you think about the world we live in?

may 5

Psalm 8:5
How close are we to God's angels?

KJV: *[God did this for us!]* For thou hast made him a little lower than the angels, and hast crowned him with glory and honour.

NISV: *[God did this for us!]* You made him a little lower than the heavenly beings and crowned him with glory and honor.

GNB: *[God did this for us!]*…Yet you made him inferior only to yourself, you crowned him with glory and honor.

TMB: *[God did this for us!]* Yet we've so narrowly missed being gods, bright with Eden's dawn light.

Thank You, Lord, for sending Your Son to free us from our sins. We praise You and honor You for what You have done for us.

may 6

Psalm 8:6–8
Who is the ruler of the universe?

KJV: *[God did this for us!]* Thou madest him to have dominion over the works of thy hands: thou hast put all *things* under his feet: ⁷ All sheep and oxen, yea, and the beasts of the field; ⁸ The fowl of the air, and the fish of the sea, and *whatsoever* passeth through the paths of the seas.

NISV: *[God did this for us!]* You made him ruler over the works of your hands; you put everything under his feet: ⁷ All flocks and herds, and the beasts of the field, ⁸ the birds of the air, and the fish of the sea, all that swim the paths of the seas.

GNB: *[God did this for us!]* You appointed him ruler over everything you made; you placed him over all creation; ⁷ sheep and cattle, and the wild animals too: ⁸ the birds and the fish and the creatures in the seas.

TMB: *[God did this for us!]* You put us in charge of your handcrafted world, repeated to us your Genesis-charge, ⁷ Made us lords of sheep and cattle, even animals out in the wild, ⁸ Birds flying and fish swimming, whales singing in the ocean deeps.

Help us remember You have made all things. Thank You for all the wonderful animals and other creatures You have put on this earth for our enjoyment. Help us to take better care of our earth. Thank You for all the miracles You performed when You created the earth.

"I Believe in Miracles" *is a hymn that tells us what God has done for us:* "Creation shows the power of God—There's glory all around, And those who see must stand in awe, For miracles abound. I believe in miracles—I've seen a soul set free, Miraculous the change in one redeemed through Calvary; I've seen the lily push its way up through the stubborn sod—I believe in miracles for I believe in God! The love of God! O power divine! Tis wonderful to see The miracle of grace performed Within the heart of me…I believe in miracles for I believe in God." Words by Carlton Buck and music by John W. Peterson.

may 7

Psalm 8:9
What is in a name?

KJV: O Lord our Lord, how excellent *is* they name in all the earth!

NISV: O Lord our Lord, how majestic is your name in all the earth!

GNB: O Lord, our Lord, your greatness is seen in all the world!

TMB: God, brilliant Lord, your name echoes around the world.

Let us praise God from whom all blessings flow. Praise His holy name!

may 8

Psalm 9:1
"Thanksgiving to God for His Justice" (GNB)

KJV: *[David cries to the Lord]*...I will praise *thee*, O LORD, with my whole heart; I will shew forth all they marvelous works.

NISV: *[David cries to the Lord]*...I will praise you, O LORD, with all my heart; I will tell of all your wonders.

GNB: *[David cries to the Lord]*...I will praise you, LORD with all my heart; I will tell of all the wonderful things you have done.

TMB: *[David cries to the Lord]*...I'm thanking you, God, from a full heart. I'm writing the book on your wonders.

How do You praise the Lord? God, Your wonders never stop amazing us. Thank You for all You have given us.

may 9

Psalm 9:2
Do you sing praises to the Lord?

- KJV: *[David says]*...I will be glad and rejoice in thee: I will sing praise to thy name, O thou most high.
- NISV: *[David says]*...I will be glad and rejoice in you; I will sing praise to your name, O Most High.
- GNB: *[David says]*...I will sing with joy because of you. I will sing praise to you Almighty God.
- TMB: *[David says]*...I'm whistling, laughing, and jumping for joy! I'm singing your song, High God.

Help us show those around us that we love them through caring for them and loving and praising You.
  Do your friends know you know the Lord?

may 10

Psalm 9:3
Who are our enemies? How do we take care of them?

KJV: *[David says]*...When mine enemies are turned back, they shall fall and perish at thy presence.

NISV: *[David says]*...My enemies turn back; they stumble and perish before you.

GNB: *[David says]*...My enemies turn back when you appear; they fall down and die.

TMB: *[David says]*...The day my enemies turned tail and ran, they stumbled on you and fell on their faces.

Help us to see who our enemies are and trust You to take care of them.

may 11

Psalm 9:4
Who is in charge of your life?

KJV: *[David talking to God]*...For thou hast maintained my right and my cause: thou satest in the throne judging right.

NISV: *[David talking to God]*...For you have upheld my right and my cause; you have sat on your throne, judging righteously.

GNB: *[David talking to God]*...You are fair and honest in your judgments, and you have judged in my favor.

TMB: *[David talking to God]*...You took over and set everything right; when I needed you, you were there, taking charge.

David believed God's judgments were fair and just.

If you allow the Lord to show *you how to settle things, you will be amazed at the outcome. Lord, help us to let You take charge and lead us in the right way.*

Who really is in charge of your life?

may 12

Psalm 9:5
Do you believe God will protect you from the evil in this world?

KJV: *[David talking to God]* Thou hast rebuked the heathen. Thou hast destroyed the wicked; thou hast put out their name for ever and ever.

NISV: *[David talking to God]* You have rebuked the nations and destroyed the wicked; you have blotted out their name for ever and ever.

GNB: *[David talking to God]* You have condemned the heathen and destroyed the wicked; they will be remembered no more.

TMB: *[David talking to God]* You blow the whistle on godless nations; you throw dirty players out of the game, wipe their names right off the roster.

The Lord will take care of those who do not obey Him like He took care of David's enemies. We are blessed with a loving God who takes care of us.

If you would like to do an in-depth study of the Bible go to http://bible.christianity.com and click on Bible in a Year. There are many sections in this web site for study.

may 13

Psalm 9:6
Will the enemies of God get away with their wicked ways?

KJV: *[God takes cares of David's enemies.]* O thou enemy, destructions are come to a perpetual end: and thou hast destroyed cities; their memorial is perished with them.

NISV: *[God did this for us!]* Endless ruin has overtaken the enemy, you have uprooted their cities; even the memory of them has perished.

GNB: *[God did this for us!]* Our enemies are finished forever, you have destroyed their cities, and they are completely forgotten.

TMB: *[God did this for us!]* Enemies disappear from the sidelines, their reputation trashed, their names erased from the halls of fame.

No one will remain untouched by the Lord's hand.

may 14

Psalm 9:7
Who can we depend on to take care of
the things in this world?

- KJV: But the LORD shall endure for ever: he hath prepared his throne for judgment.
- NISV: The LORD reigns forever; he has established his throne for judgment.
- GNB: But the LORD is king forever; he has set up his throne for judgment.
- TMB: God holds the high center, he sees and sets the world's mess right.

God! Thank You for taking care of many unseen things that would harm us.

may 15

Psalm 9:8
On which side of justice are you?

KJV: *[The Lord will reign.]* And he shall judge the world in righteousness, he shall minister judgment to the people in uprightness.

NISV: *[The Lord will reign.]* He will judge the world in righteousness; he will govern the people with justice.

GNB: *[The Lord will reign.]* He rules the world with righteousness; he judges the nations with justice.

TMB: *[The Lord will reign.]* He decides what is right for us earthlings, gives people their just deserts.

Are you ready to stand before God as you are?

may 16

Psalm 9:9
Where do you turn for help?

KJV: The Lord also will be a refuge for the oppressed, a refuge in times of trouble.

NISV: The Lord is a refuge for the oppressed, a stronghold in times of trouble.

GNB: The Lord is a refuge for the oppressed, a place of safety in times of trouble.

TMB: God's a safe-house for the battered, a sanctuary during bad times.

"A Mighty Fortress Is Our God" *a hymn written in the 1600s is still true today. Words and music by Martin Luther.* A mighty fortress is our God, A bulwark never failing; Our helper He, amid the flood Of mortal ills prevailing: For still our ancient foe Doth seek to work us woe; His craft and power are great,…His kingdom is forever.

The Lord is there to help us; all we need to do is ask.

may 17

Psalm 9:10
Have you told anyone lately what the
Lord can do for them?

KJV: *[David said]*...And they that know thy name will put their trust in thee: for thou, LORD, hast not forsaken them that seek thee.

NISV: *[David said]*...Those who know your name will trust in you, for you, LORD, have never forsaken those who seek you.

GNB: *[David said]*...Those who know you, LORD, will trust you; you do not abandon anyone who comes to you.

TMB: *[David said]*...The moment you arrive, you relax; You're never sorry you knocked.

What do your friends think you believe?

may 18

Psalm 9:11
Do your friends know that you know Jesus?

KJV: Sing praises to the LORD, which dwelleth in Zion: declare among the people his doings.

NISV: Sing praises to the LORD, enthroned in Zion; proclaim among the nations what he has done.

GNB: Sing praise to the LORD, who rules in Zion! Tell every nation what he has done!

TMB: Sing your songs to Zion-dwelling God, tell his stories to everyone you meet:

We love to praise the Lord in prayer and song. Let's tell others how Jesus loves us by sharing His word with them.

"Praise Him! Praise Him!" Words by Fanny J Crosby and music by Chester G. Allen. Fanny Crosby is one of the world most famous gospel song writers. *The words of this song express everything we need to know about God.*

Praise Him! Praise Him! Jesus, our blessed Redeemer! Sing, O earth-His wonderful love proclaim! Hail Him! Hail Him! Highest archangels in glory, Strength and honor give to His holy name! Like a shepherd Jesus will guard His children- In His arms He carries them all day long: Praise Him! Praise Him! Tell of His excellent greatness! Praise Him! Praise Him! Ever in joyful song.

may 19

Psalm 9:12
Does God know what we do? Does he care about our pain?

KJV: *[David said God takes cares of us.]* When he maketh inquisition for blood, he remembereth them: he forgetteth not the cry of the humble.

NISV: *[David said God takes cares of us.]* For he who avenges blood remembers; he does not ignore the cry of the afflicted.

GNB: God remembers those who suffer; he does not forget their cry, and he punishes those who wrong them.

TMB: *[David said God will take care of us.]* How he tracks down killers yet keeps his eye on us, registers every whimper and moan.

Yes, God loves us and keeps track of our every move.

may 20

Psalm 9:13
Have you accepted God's grace and peace?

KJV: *[David cried to God]*...Have mercy upon me, O Lord; consider my trouble *which I suffer* of them that hate me, thou that liftest me up from the gates of death:

NISV: *[David cried to God]*...O Lord, see how my enemies persecute me! Have mercy and lift me up from the gates of death,

GNB: *[David cried to God]*...Be merciful to me, O Lord! See the sufferings my enemies cause me! Rescue me from death, O Lord!

TMB: *[David cried to God]*...Be kind to me, God; I've been kicked around long enough. Once you've pulled me back from the gates of death,

The Lord sees all things; He knows when we need help. God is watching over us. He wants us to ask for His guidance and mercy.

may 21

Psalm 9:14
Do we let our praises be heard?

KJV: *[David singing praises to God]* That I may show forth all thy praise in the gates of the daughter of Zion; I will rejoice in thy salvation.

NISV: *[David singing praises to God]*...that I may declare your praises in the gates of the Daughter of Zion and there rejoice in your salvation.

GNB: *[David singing praises to God]*...that I may stand before the people of Jerusalem and tell them all the things for which I praise you. I will rejoice because you saved me.

TMB: *[David singing praises to God]*...I'll write the book on Hallelujahs; on the corner of Main and First. I'll hold a street meeting; I'll be the song leader; we'll fill the air with salvation songs.

The only way God knows how we appreciate Him is by our worship, praise, and prayers. The song "Awesome God" praises the Lord in wonderful words. Part of the song says,

"Our God is an awesome God, He reigns from heaven above with wisdom, power, and love. Our God is an awesome God." "Awesome God" by Rich Mullins, composer and lyrics.

Thank You, Lord, for the songs given through You to musicians that help us express ourselves.

may 22

Psalm 9:15
What and where can we hide from God?

- KJV: *[David talking about the people who are chasing him.]* The heathen are sunk down in the pit that they made; in the net which they hide is their own foot taken.
- NISV: *[David talking about the people who are chasing him.]* The nations have fallen into the pit they have dug; their feet are caught in the net they have hidden.
- GNB: *[David talking about the people who are chasing him.]* The heathen have dug a pit and fallen in: they have been caught in their own trap.
- TMB: *[David talking about the people who are chasing him.]* They're trapped, those godless countries, in the very snares they set. Their feet all tangled in the net they spread.

The people in the world think no one is watching! But God governs everything; those who don't pay attention will not be happy in the end.

may 23

Psalm 9:16
Who do drug dealers think they are kidding?

KJV: *[From the psalmist.]* The LORD is known by the judgment *which* he executeth: the wicked is snared in the work of his own hands. Higgaion, Selah.

NISV: *[From the psalmist.]* The LORD is known by his justice; the wicked are ensnared by the work of their hands. Higgaion. Selah

GNB: *[From the psalmist.]* The LORD has revealed himself by his righteous judgments, and the wicked are trapped by their own deeds.

TMB: *[From the psalmist.]* They have no excuse; the way God works is well-known. The cunning machinery made by the wicked has maimed their own hands.

The things that are made by human hands that destroy people's lives will come to a bitter end.

may 24

Psalm 9:17
Do you tell those who do not know the
Lord how He helps you each day?

- KJV: *[David talking about the people who are chasing him.]* The wicked shall be turned into hell, all the nations that forget God.

- NISV: *[David talking about the people who are chasing him.]* The wicked return to the grave, all the nations that forget God.

- GNB: *[David talking about the people who are chasing him.]* Death is the destiny of all the wicked, of all those who reject God.

- TMB: *[David talking about the people who are chasing him.]* The wicked bought a one-way ticket to hell.

We need to warn the "wicked" among us. If we don't share the good news of Christ's saving power, who will?

Heaven Is Real Do You Have Reservations? (From magnet M-110 c Big M Graphics.)

may 25

Psalm 9:18
Have you helped anyone in need?

KJV: *[David talking about the people that need help from God.]* For the needy shall not always be forgotten: the expectation of the poor shall *not* perish for ever.

NISV: *[David talking about the people that need help from God.]* But the needy will not always be forgotten, nor the hope of the afflicted ever perish.

GNB: *[David talking about the people that need help from God.]* The needy will not always be neglected; the hope of the poor will not be crushed forever.

TMB: *[David talking about the people that need help from God.]* No longer will the poor be nameless—no more humiliation for the humble.

When we share what we have with others, we receive more than we give.

may 26

Psalm 9:19
Does God work fast enough for you?

- KJV: *[David talking about the people that are disobeying God.]* Arise, O LORD; let not man prevail: let the heathen be judged in they sight.
- NISV: *[David talking about the people that are disobeying God.]* Arise, O LORD, let not man triumph; let the nations be judged in your presence.
- GNB: *[David talking about the people that are disobeying God.]* Come, LORD! Do not let men defy you! Bring the heathen before you and pronounce judgment on them.
- TMB: *[David talking about the people that are disobeying God.]* Up, God! Aren't you fed up with their empty strutting? Expose these grand pretensions!

We need patience! Help us to accept that God's timing is perfect.

may 27

Psalm 9:20
What makes you afraid of believing in Jesus?

KJV: *[David cried to God...]* Put them in fear, O LORD; *that* the nations may know themselves *to be* but men. Selah.

NISV: *[David cried to God...]* Strike them with terror, O LORD; let the nations know they are but men. *Selah*

GNB: *[David cried to God...]* Make them afraid, O LORD; make them know that they are only mortal beings.

TMB: *[David cried to God...]* Shake them up, God! Show them how silly they look.

God will take care of those who boast and think there is no judgment day coming.

The Lord is waiting to hear from you. He is not the enemy. He wants to give peace. He is the only God that can bring peace to your mind and soul. Ask Him to come into your life and save you from your sins. You don't have to wait for a special time or day. He is always near and will hear your prayer. He wants you to join His family.

may 28

Psalm 10:1
"A Prayer for Justice" (GNB)

The chapter of Psalm 10 from The Message Bible is on June 18.

KJV: *[David cried to God...]* Why standest thou afar off, O LORD: why hidest thou thy self in times of trouble?

NISV: *[David cried to God...]* Why, O LORD, do you stand far off? Why do you hide yourself in times of trouble?

GNB: *[David cried to God...]* Why are you so far away, O LORD? Why do you hide yourself when we are in trouble?

TMB: *[David cried to God...]* God, are you avoiding me? Where are you when I need you?

The United States has had many hurricanes and tornadoes in the past years. Many news reporters talk to people that have come through the experience and lost everything but their families. Many tell their stories and then say how God has blessed them and saved their families.

Lord, help us to remember You never said living on this earth would be easy, but You promised to be with us in every situation and give us comfort and hope.

Has the Lord answered your prayers lately?

If you don't have a prayer box, get a box and cut a hole

in the top. Decorate the box if you like. Write down your prayer requests on a slip of paper and put them in the box. Check it weekly or monthly and see how your prayers are being answered.

may 29

Psalm 10:2
"A Prayer for Justice" (GNB)

KJV: The wicked in his pride doth persecute the poor; let them be taken in the devices that they have imagined.

NISV: In his arrogance the wicked man hunts down the weak, who are caught in the schemes he devises.

GNB: The wicked are proud and persecute the poor; catch them in the traps they have made.

TMB: Full of hot air, the wicked are hot on the trail of the poor. Trip them up, tangle them up in their fine-tuned plots.

When our feelings get hurt and we need to say we forgive someone, it is a hard thing to do. But when you go to the person and take care of the problem, you will feel so much better. God will help you forgive and forget—just like God forgives and forgets our sins.

Does your pride get in the way of what the Lord wants you to do?

may 30

Psalm 10:3
"A Prayer for Justice" (GNB)

KJV: *[The psalmist talks about the wicked.]* For the wicked boasteth of his heart's desire, and blesseth the covetous, *whom* the LORD abhorreth.

NISV: *[The psalmist talks about the wicked.]* He boasts of the cravings of his heart; he blesses the greedy and reviles the LORD.

GNB: *[The psalmist talks about the wicked.]* The wicked man is proud of his evil desires; the greedy man curses and rejects the LORD.

TMB: *[The psalmist talks about the wicked.]* The wicked are windbags, the swindlers have foul breath.

If the world can capture our heart and turn it toward coveting worldly possessions, our relationship with God will soon be disrupted. God wants us to worship Him only.
  What is your heart's desire?

may 31

Psalm 10:4
"A Prayer for Justice" (GNB)

KJV: *[The psalmist talks about the wicked.]* The wicked, through the pride of his countenance, will not seek after God: God is not in all his thoughts.

NISV: *[The psalmist talks about the wicked.]* In his pride the wicked does not seek him; in all his thoughts there is not room for God.

GNB: *[The psalmist talks about the wicked.]* A wicked man does not care about the LORD: in his pride he thinks that God doesn't matter.

TMB: *[The psalmist talks about the wicked.]* The wicked snub God, their noses stuck high in the air. Their graffiti are scrawled on the walls: "Catch us if you can!" "God is dead."

God wants the corner on our every thought. He is a jealous God and wants us to love only Him. If people hurt you or your "pride," don't let it get to you. He understands how bad people can make you feel. Pray and God will help you handle it.

In what way does pride rule your life?

june 1

Psalm 10:5
"A Prayer for Justice" (GNB)

KJV: *[The psalmist talks about the wicked.]* His ways are always grievous; thy judgments are far above out of his sight: as for all his enemies, he puffeth at them.

NISV: *[The psalmist talks about the wicked.]* His ways are always prosperous; he is haughty and your laws are far from him; he sneers at all his enemies.

GNB: *[The psalmist talks about the wicked.]* A wicked man succeeds in everything. He cannot understand God's judgments; he sneers at his enemies.

TMB: *[The psalmist talks about the wicked.]* They care nothing for what you think; if you get in their way, they blow you off.

The man who says God does not exist will have an enormous wake-up call when he or she has to answer to the Lord. American people are questioning why God is allowing all the destruction in our country. We have treated God so badly and the phrase "God Bless America" is so trivialized that people just say it without knowing what they mean. Instead of just saying good-bye, the phrase "God Bless America" is rather flippant and without meaning. The phrase should remind us that God is in the universe and can bless our country if we do His will.

june 2

Psalm 10:6
"A Prayer for Justice" (GNB)

KJV: *[This is what the people that are lost from God think.]* He hath said in his heart, I shall not be moved; for I shall never be in adversity.

NISV: *[This is what the people that are lost from God think.]* He says to himself, "Nothing will shake me; I'll always be happy and never have trouble."

GNB: *[This is what the people that are lost from God think.]* He says to himself, "I will never fail; I will never be in trouble."

TMB: *[This is what the people that are lost from God think.]* They live (they think) a charmed life: "We can't go wrong. This is our lucky year!"

The sinner who thinks that he will never fail had better look around. If you don't believe that Jesus came to save us, it is time for you to take that step. Let the Lord into your life. He is the only "God" that can give you peace.

What is your heart longing for?

Browse Dr. Dobson's website: http://oneplace.com. Dr. Dobson is the radio host for Focus on the Family.

june 3

Psalm 10:7
"A Prayer for Justice" (GNB)

KJV: *[Some people who don't know God are like this.]* His mouth is full of cursing and deceit and fraud: under his tongue is mischief and vanity.

NISV: *[Some people who don't know God are like this.]* His mouth is full of curses and lies and threats; trouble and evil are under his tongue.

GNB: *[Some people who don't know God are like this.]* His speech is filled with curses, lies and threats; he is quick to speak hateful evil words.

TMB: *[Some people who don't know God are like this.]* They carry a mouthful of hexes, their tongues spit venom like adders.

People who have no vocabulary but four-letter words should make us feel uncomfortable. The terms they use are worthless and only let you know that they don't know any better. The nasty words that come from people's mouths give us a great clue to their inner feelings and sad look at the world. God can lift us up and fill our lives with meaningful words and thoughts.

What do you think people who hear you speak think of your background?

june 4

Psalm 10:8
"A Prayer for Justice" (GNB)

KJV: *[Some people who don't know God are like this.]* He sitteth in the lurking places of the villages: in the secret places doth he murder the innocent: his eyes are privily set against the poor.

NISV: *[Some people who don't know God are like this.]* He lies in wait near the villages; from ambush he murders the innocent, watching in secret for his victims.

GNB: *[Some people who don't know God are like this.]* He hides himself in the villages waiting to murder innocent people. He spies on his helpless victims.

TMB: *[Some people who don't know God are like this.]* They hide behind ordinary people, then pounce on their victims;

The villains in this world who prey on innocent people will always pay in the end. God sees what each and every one of us does. We can't hide anything from Him. Make it easy on yourself, do it God's way and you will come out on top.

june 5

Psalm 10:9
"A Prayer for Justice" (GNB)

KJV: *[Some people who don't know God are like this.]* He lieth in wait secretly as a lion in his den: he lieth in wait to catch the poor: he doth catch the poor, when he draweth him into his net.

NISV: *[Some people who don't know God are like this.]* He lies in wait like a lion in cover; he lies in wait to catch the helpless; he catches the helpless and drags them off in his net.

GNB: *[Some people who don't know God are like this.]*…he waits in his hiding place like a lion. He lies in wait for the poor; he catches them in his trap and drags them away.

TMB: *[Some people who don't know God are like this.]* They mark the luckless, then wait like a hunter in a blind; When the poor wretch wanders too close, they stab him in the back.

If we are praying that the Lord will watch over us and protect us, we can trust Him to get us through every situation.

june 6

Psalm 10:10
"A Prayer for Justice" (GNB)

KJV: *[Some people who don't know God do these things.]* He croucheth; and humbleth himself, that the poor may fall by his strong ones.

NISV: *[Some people who don't know God do these things.]* His victims are crushed, they collapse; they fall under his strength.

GNB: *[Some people who don't know God do these things.]* The helpless victims lie crushed; brute strength has defeated them.

TMB: *[Some people who don't know God do these things.]* The hapless fool is kicked to the ground, the unlucky victim is brutally axed.

Those who don't follow the Lord can't realize the miracles He will perform to protect us. Help us to tell our friends about the miracles and blessings we have seen and experienced as talked about in this song.

"When upon life's billows you are tempest-tossed, When you are discouraged, thinking all is lost, Count your many blessings-name them one by one, And it will surprise you what the Lord hath done....Are you ever burdened with a load of care? Does the cross seem heavy you are called to bear/ Count your many blessings-name them one by one, And it will surprise you what the Lord hath done….When you look at others with their land and gold, Think that Christ has promised you His wealth untold; Count your many blessings money cannot buy Your reward in heaven nor your home on high. Count your blessings name them one by one…Count your many blessings-see what God hath done."

"Count Your Blessings" words by Johnson Oatman, Jr. music by Edwin O. Excell.

june 7

Psalm 10:11
"A Prayer for Justice" (GNB)

KJV: *[Some people who don't know God say this.]* He hath said in his heart, God hath forgotten: he hideth his face; he will never see it.

NISV: *[Some people who don't know God say this.]* He says to himself, "God has forgotten he covers his face and never sees."

GNB: *[Some people who don't know God say this.]* The wicked man says to himself, "God doesn't care! He has closed his eyes and will never see me!"

TMB: *[Some people who don't know God say this.]* He thinks God has dumped him, he's sure that God is indifferent to this plight.

The man who thinks he has gotten away with "murder" is fooled by his mixed up mind.

Romans 12:19: "Do not take revenge, my friends, but leave room for God's wrath, for it is written: 'It is mine to avenge, I will repay.' Says the LORD" (NISV).

june 8

Psalm 10:12
"A Prayer for Justice" (GNB)

KJV: *[The psalmist pleads with God for the lonely and forgotten.]* Arise, O LORD; O God, life up thine hand: forget not the humble.

NISV: *[The psalmist pleads with God for the lonely and forgotten.]* Arise, LORD! Lift up your hand, O God. Do not forget the helpless.

GNB: *[The psalmist pleads with God for the lonely and forgotten.]* O LORD, punish those wicked men! Remember those who are suffering!

TMB: *[The psalmist pleads with God for the lonely and forgotten.]* Time to get up, God—get moving. The luckless think they're Godforsaken.

God is always available. He is here waiting for your request for help. Call upon Him; He will hear you and answer your prayers.

What has God done for you lately? What do you want Him to do for you?

june 9

Psalm 10:13
"A Prayer for Justice" (GNB)

KJV: *[Where is justice?]* Wherefore doth the wicked contemn God? He hath said in his heart, Thou wilt not require it.

NISV: *[Where is justice?]* Why does the wicked man revile God: Why does he say to himself, "He won't call me to account"?

GNB: *[Where is justice?]* How can a wicked man despise God, and say to himself, "He will not punish me"?

TMB: *[Where is justice?]* They wonder why the wicked scorn God and get away with it, why the wicked are so cocksure they'll never come up for audit.

The 2005 hurricane season had been full of surprises. Around the world we are hearing of many natural disasters. People are talking. Is the Lord sending us a message that He is tired of the world's lack of attention to Him? We think we are special and He is protecting those who call on His name. Many people have ignored what the Lord has been telling them. We do have free will. Will our free will lead to our demise? Lord, we hope this country will pay attention and turn back to You.

june 10

Psalm 10:14
"A Prayer for Justice" (GNB)

KJV: *[Where is God's justice?]* Thou hast seen *it;* for thou beholdest mischief and spite, to requite it with thy hand: the poor committeth himself unto thee; thou are the helper of the fatherless.

NISV: *[Where is God's justice?]* But you, O God, do see trouble and grief; you consider it to take it in hand. The victim commits himself to you; you are the helper of the fatherless.

GNB: *[Where is God's justice?]* But you do see; you take notice of trouble and suffering and are always ready to help. The helpless man commits himself to you; you have always helped the needy.

TMB: *[Where is God's justice?]* But you know all about it—the contempt, the abuse. I dare to believe that the luckless will get lucky someday in you. You won't let them down: orphans won't be orphans forever.

God's justice will come to those who don't obey Him when the time is right in His eyes. We know whatever storm or trial we go through the Lord is our strength and shield.

june 11

Psalm 10:15
"A Prayer for Justice" (GNB)

KJV: *[Lord]* Break thou the arm of the wicked and the evil man: seek out his wickedness till thou find none.

NISV: *[Lord]* Break the arm of the wicked and evil man; call him to account for his wickedness that would not be found out.

GNB: *[Lord]* Break the power of wicked and evil men; punish them for the wrong they have done until they do it no more.

TMB: *[Lord]* Break the wicked right arms, break all the evil left arms. Search and destroy every sign of crime.

Many new storms have hit New Orleans since Katrina, with flooding and damage. Will the rebuilding of the "most corrupt" [quoted from CNN] city in our country take place? Are the prophesies of Revelation starting to be revealed to us? We need to help our friends find peace with God.

Lord, help us to be what You want us to be.

june 12

Psalm 10:16
"A Prayer for Justice" (GNB)

KJV: The Lord is King for ever and ever: the heathen are perished out of his land.

NISV: The Lord is King for ever and ever; the nations will perish from his land.

GNB: The Lord is king forever and ever. Those who worship other gods will vanish from this land.

TMB: God's grace and order wins; godlessness loses.

Help us to know Your grace and peace. Help us to help others know You.

Our only hope is in the Lord because we know that whatever happens the Savior is waiting to take care of us. This song reminds us how wonderful God can be.

"He's a wonderful Savior to me. For He's a wonderful Savior to me…I was lost in sin but Jesus rescued me…I was bound by fear but Jesus set me free…He's a Friend so true, so patient and so kind…Everything I need in Him I always find…He is always near to comfort and to cheer.… He forgives my sins, He dries my every tear…Sweeter is His grace while pressing on my way, For he's a wonderful Savior to me."

"He's a Wonderful Saviour to Me" words by Virgil P. Brock music by Blanche Kerr Brock

june 13

Psalm 10:17
"A Prayer for Justice" (GNB)

KJV: Lord, thou hast heard the desire of the humble: thou wilt prepare their heart, thou with cause thine ear to hear:

NISV: You hear, O Lord, the desire of the afflicted; you encourage them and you listen to their cry.

GNB: You will listen, O Lord, to the prayers of the lowly; you will give them courage.

TMB: The victim's faint pulse picks up; the hearts of the hopeless pump red blood as you put your ear to their lips.

Dear Lord, we pray you are with all the refugees from the natural disasters in America and around the world. Help us realize how important You are in our lives. You are the one "possession" we can keep in our hearts, and no one can take You away from us.

Thank You for Your love, compassion, and grace every day.
How do you show compassion to your friends?

june 14

Psalm 10:18
"A Prayer for Justice" (GNB)

KJV: *[The psalmist is asking the Lord to help these people.]* To judge the fatherless and the oppressed; that the man of the earth may no more oppress.

NISV: *[The psalmist is asking the Lord to help these people.]* ... defending the fatherless and the oppressed, in order that man, who is of the earth, may terrify no more.

GNB: *[The psalmist is asking the Lord to help these people.]* You will hear the cries of the oppressed and the orphans; you will judge in their favor, so that mortal men may cause terror no more.

TMB: *[The psalmist is asking the Lord to help these people.]* Orphans get parents, the homeless get homes. The reign of terror is over, the rule of the gang lords is ended.

We have seen so many deaths and people made homeless by the earthquakes in Pakistan, China, and the cyclone that devastated Myanmar. The only hope they have is to be rescued by miracles of kindness. We as Christians must lead the way and help people such as these in every way possible. If we can't give money or things, our prayers will reach to heaven as the Lord performs His miracles in ways we will never know.

We have read a verse each day from May 28 to June 14, on the next page is the chapter from Psalm 10:1–18, TMB.

"A Prayer for Justice"

God, are you avoiding me? Where are you when I need you? Full of hot air, the wicked are hot on the trail of the poor. Trip them up, tangle them up in their fine-tuned plots. The wicked are windbags, the swindlers have foul breath. The wicked snub God, their noses stuck high in the air. Their graffiti are scrawled on the wall: "Catch us if you can!" "God is dead." They care nothing for what you think; If you get in their way, they blow you off. They live (they think) a charmed life; "We can't go wrong. This is our lucky year!" They carry a mouthful of hexes, their tongues spit venom like adders. They hide behind ordinary people, then pounce on their victims. They mark the luckless, then wait like a hunter in a blind; When the poor wretch wanders too close, they stab him in the back. The hapless fool is kicked to the ground, the unlucky victim is brutally axed. He thinks God has dumped him, he's sure that God is indifferent to his plight. Time to get up, God—get moving; The luckless think they're Godforsaken. They wonder why the wicked scorn God and get away with it, Why the wicked are so cocksure they'll never come up for audit. But you know all about it—the contempt, the abuse. I dare to believe that the luckless will get lucky someday in you. You won't let them down: orphans won't be orphans forever. Break the wicked right arms, break all the evil left arms. Search and destroy every sign of crime. God's grace and order wins; godlessness loses. The victim's faint pulse picks up; the hearts of the hopeless pump red blood as you put your ear to their lips. Orphans get parents, the homeless get homes. The reign of terror is over, the rule of the gang lords is ended.

june 15

Psalm 11:1 (GNB)
We have confidence in the Lord.

The entire chapter of Psalm 11 from The Message Bible is on June 21.

KJV: In the LORD I put my trust: how-say ye to my soul. Flee as a bird to your mountain?

NISV: In the LORD I take refuge. How then can you say to me: "Flee like a bird to your mountain.

GNB: I trust in the LORD for safety. How foolish of you to say to me. "Fly away like a bird to the mountains…"

TMB: I've already run for dear life straight to the arms of God. So why would I run away now when you say…Run to the mountains…

When we put our trust in the Lord, we do not have to run to the mountains. He will find us wherever we are and meet our needs.

To learn more about the Bible go to: http://bible.christianity.com

june 16

Psalm 11:2
We have confidence in the Lord.

KJV: *[David praying for mercy]*…For, lo, the wicked bend their bow, they make ready their arrow upon the string, that they may privily shoot at the upright in heart.

NISV: *[David praying for mercy]*…For look, the wicked bend their bows; they set their arrows against the strings to shoot from the shadows at the upright in heart.

GNB: *[David praying for mercy]*…because the wicked have drawn their bows and aimed their arrows to shoot at good men in the darkness.

TMB: *[David praying for mercy]*…"Run to the mountains, the evil bows are bent, the wicked arrows aimed to shoot under cover of darkness at every heart open to God…

Sometimes the arrows that are pointed at us are words that are not true and are very damaging and hurtful. God didn't say things would always be sunny and perfect. He does say He will protect us and help us get through the bad times. He is always with us.

Thank You, Lord, for Your protection and care.

june 17

Psalm 11:3
We have confidence in the Lord.

kjv: *[David praying for mercy]*...If the foundations be destroyed, what can the righteous do?

nisv: *[David praying for mercy]*..."When the foundations are being destroyed, what can the righteous do"?

gnb: *[David praying for mercy]*...There is nothing a good man can do when everything falls apart."

tmb: *[David praying for mercy]*..."The bottom's dropped out of the country; good people don't have a chance"?

No! We don't have a chance unless we ask God to help us. He alone can take care of catastrophic times. He will come to our rescue if we ask Him to.

Has God rescued you when you thought you had lost everything?

june 18

Psalm 11:4
We have confidence in the Lord.

KJV: The Lord is in his holy temple, the Lord's throne is in heaven: his eyes behold, his eyelids try, the children of men.

NISV: The Lord is in his holy temple, the Lord is on his heavenly throne. He observes the sons of men; his eyes examine them.

GNB: The Lord is in his holy temple; he has his throne in heaven. He watches people everywhere and knows what they are doing.

TMB: But God hasn't moved to the mountains; his holy address hasn't changed. He's in charge as always, his eyes taking everything in, his eyelids Unblinking, examining Adam's unruly brood inside and out, not missing a thing.

It is hard for us to imagine how God can see and know everything. Lucky for us, He is not human. We don't have to comprehend His ways; we only have to trust Him to take care of us.

june 19

Psalm 11:5
We have confidence in the Lord.

KJV: The LORD trieth the righteous, but the wicked and him that loveth violence his soul hateth.

NISV: The LORD examines the righteous, but the wicked and those who love violence his soul hates.

GNB: He examines the good and the wicked alike; the lawless he hates with all his heart.

TMB: He tests the good and the bad alike; if anyone cheats, God's outraged.

We are tested in many ways. The Lord knows our hearts. We should love, serve, and praise Him in outward ways that show we are committed to do His will. Jesus will be with us and acknowledge us before our heavenly Father.

june 20

Psalm 11:6
We have confidence in the Lord.

KJV: *[David is talking about what will happen to non-worshippers.]* Upon the wicked he shall rain snares, fire and brimstone, and an horrible tempest: *this shall* be the portion of their cup.

NISV: *[David is talking about what will happen to non-worshippers.]* On the wicked he will rain fiery coals and burning sulfur; a scorching wind will be their lot.

GNB: *[David is talking about what will happen to non-worshippers.]* He sends down flaming coals and burning sulfur on the wicked; he punishes them with scorching winds.

TMB: *[David is talking about what will happen to non-worshippers.]* Fail the test and you're out, out in a hail of firestones, Drinking from a canteen filled with hot desert wind.

Those who do not serve and please the Lord will pay dearly when He gets tired of their ways. I would rather serve the Lord now than pay later.

june 21

Psalm 11:7
We have confidence in the Lord.

KJV: For the righteous LORD loveth righteousness; his countenance doth behold the upright.

NISV: For the LORD is righteous he loves justice; upright men will see his face.

GNB: The LORD is righteous and loves good deeds: those who do them will live in his presence.

TMB: God's business is putting things right; he loves getting the lines straight. Setting us straight. Once we're standing tall, we can look him straight in the eye.

We have read a verse each day from June 15 to 21; below is Psalm 11 from The Message Bible.
Psalm 11

I've already run for dear life straight to the arms of God. So why would I run away now when you say, "Run to the mountains; the evil bows are bent, the wicked arrows aimed to shoot under cover of darkness at every heart open to God. "The bottom's dropped out of the country; good people don't have a chance"? But God hasn't moved to the mountains; his holy address hasn't changed. He's in charge, as always, his eyes taking everything in, his eyelids unblinking, examining Adam's unruly brood inside and out, not missing a thing. He tests the good and the bad alike; if anyone cheats, God's outraged. Fail the test and you're out, out in a hail of firestones, Drinking from a canteen filled with hot desert wind. God's business is putting things right. He loves getting the lines straight. Setting us straight. Once we're standing tall, we can look Him straight in the eye.

Will you be ready to look the Lord in the eye when He comes? Can He say to you, "You loved me, kept my commandments, and asked for forgiveness of your sins"? If you're worried about what comes at the end of your life, now is the time to turn your life over to Him and let Him run it. Just ask Him to forgive you of your sins and come into your heart. He will bless you.

june 22

Psalm 12:1
"A Prayer for Help" (GNB)

The chapter from Psalm 12 The Message Bible is on June 29.

KJV: *[The psalmist is talking about what will happen to non-worshippers.]* Help, LORD; for the godly man ceaseth; for the faithful fall from among the children of men.

NISV: *[The psalmist is talking about what will happen to non-worshippers.]* Help, LORD, for the godly are no more; the faithful have vanished from among men.

GNB: *[The psalmist is talking about what will happen to non-worshippers.]* Help us, LORD! There is not a good man left; honest men can no longer be found.

TMB: *[The psalmist is talking about what will happen to non-worshippers.]* Quick God, I need your helping hand! The last decent person just went down, All the friends I depended on gone.

Christians are being attacked by people verbally in everyday encounters and through the media. It is hard to understand the hate that Satan has put in the hearts of men and women. We know God will stand by us and help us through every situation. Thank You, Lord, for this assurance.

june 23

Psalm 12:2
"A Prayer for Help" (GNB)

KJV: *[The psalmist is talking about deceitful people.]* They speak vanity every one with his neighbor; *with* flattering lips *and* with a double heart do they speak.

NISV: *[The psalmist is talking about deceitful people.]* Everyone lies to his neighbor; their flattering lips speak with deception.

GNB: *[The psalmist is talking about deceitful people.]* All of them lie to one another they deceive each other with flattery.

TMB: *[The psalmist is talking about deceitful people.]* Everyone talks in lie language; Lies slide off their oily lips. They doubletalk with forked tongues.

Watch out for people who don't know how to tell the truth. Their mixed up minds will mix you up. Watch your own mouth so that you do not try to deceive your friends. Lead them to a relationship with Jesus by your witness.

june 24

Psalm 12:3
"A Prayer for Help" (GNB)

KJV: *[The psalmist is requesting assistance from the Lord.]* The LORD shall cut off all flattering lips, and tongue that speaketh proud things.

NISV: *[The psalmist is requesting assistance from the Lord.]* May the LORD cut off all flattering lips and every boastful tongue

GNB: *[The psalmist is requesting assistance from the Lord.]* Silence those flattering tongues, O LORD! Close those boastful mouths that say,...

TMB: *[The psalmist is requesting assistance from the Lord.]* Slice their lips off their faces! Pull the braggart tongues from their mouths!

There is little we can do about the people around us who do not tell the truth. Just turn the problem over to Jesus. He will set it straight.

june 25

Psalm 12:4
"A Prayer for Help" (GNB)

KJV: *[The psalmist is talking about the wicked people.]* Who have said, with our tongue will we prevail; our lips are our own: who is lord over us?

NISV: *[The psalmist is talking about the wicked people.]* (Beware of him)...that says, "We will triumph with our tongues; we own our lips-who is our master?

GNB: *[The psalmist is talking about the wicked people.]* "With our words we get what we want. We will say what we wish, and no one can stop us."

TMB: *[The psalmist is talking about the wicked people.]* I'm tired of hearing, "We can talk anyone into anything! Our lips manage the world."

People talk big, say mean things, and think they can get away with it. They don't care who they hurt. Our mouths need to be controlled. God is the only one that can help us stop saying nasty things and hurting others. Lord, help us to think before we speak.

june 26

Psalm 12:5
"A Prayer for Help" (GNB)

KJV: For the oppression of the poor, for the sighing of the needy, now will I arise, saith the Lord I will set him in safety from him that puffeth at him.

NISV: Because of the oppression of the weak and the groaning of the needy, I will now arise, says the Lord. "I will protect them from those who malign them."

GNB: "But now I will come," says the Lord. "Because the needy are oppressed and the persecuted groan in pain. I will give them the security they long for."

TMB: Into the hovels of the poor, into the dark streets where the homeless groan, God Speaks: "I've had enough; I'm on my way. To heal the ache in the heart of the wretched."

Lord, thank You for taking care of Your children who don't have anyone to care for them. Help us to be more aware of their situations and show us what we need to do to help them.

Browse the Focus on the Family website. www.focusonthefamily.com for new ways of taking care of your family and children.

june 27

Psalm 12:6
"A Prayer for Help" (GNB)

KJV: The words of the LORD are pure words: as silver tried in a furnace of earth, purified seven times.

NISV: And the words of the LORD are flawless, like silver refined in a furnace of clay, purified seven times.

GNB: The promises of the LORD can be trusted; they are as genuine as silver refined seven times in the furnace.

TMB: God's words are pure words, Pure silver words refine seven times In the fires of his word-kiln, Pure on earth as well as in heaven.

Thank You, Lord, for Your true and wonderful promises to us. Help us learn more about them as we read Your word daily.

june 28

Psalm 12:7
"A Prayer for Help" (GNB)

KJV: *[The psalmist asking God to take care of His people.]* Thou shalt keep them, O Lord, thou shalt preserve them from this generation for ever.

NISV: O Lord, you will keep us safe and protect us from such people for ever.

GNB: *[The psalmist asking God to take care of His people.]* Wicked men are everywhere and everyone praises what is evil.

TMB: God, keep us safe from their lies, from the wicked who stalk us with lies…

Remember God loves us and wants to protect us. Let him come into your life and stay in your life. He will give you peace. He is the best true friend you will ever have.

june 29

Psalm 12:8
"A Prayer for Help" (GNB)

KJV: *[The psalmist asking the Lord to protect His people.]* The wicked walk on every side, when the vilest men are exalted.

NISV: *[The psalmist asking the Lord to protect His people.]* The wicked freely strut about when what is vile is honored among men.

GNB: *[The psalmist asking the Lord to protect His people.]* Keep us always safe, O Lord, and preserve us from such people.

TMB: *[The psalmist asking the Lord to protect His people.]* From the wicked who collect honors for their wonderful lies.

Lord, help us realize that You will take care of the wicked and evil people that Satan is deceiving. Thank You, Lord, for Your grace and comforting peace. Help us who have a personal relationship with You to find others and lead them to Your peace.

We have read a verse each day from June 22–29. Below is the chapter from Psalm 12 from The Message Bible. Read it to get the feel and understanding of the whole chapter.

Quick, God, I need your helping hand! The last decent person just went down. All the friends I depended on gone. Everyone talks in lie language; Lies slide off their oily lips. They doubletalk with forked tongues. Slice the lips off their faces! Pull the braggart tongues from their mouths! I'm tired of hearing, "We can talk anyone into anything! Our lips manage the world." Into the hovels of the poor, into the dark streets where the homeless groan, God Speaks: "I've had enough; I'm on my way to heal the ache in the heart of the wretched." God's words are pure words. Pure silver words refined seven times In the fires of his word-kiln; pure on earth as well as in heaven. God, keep us safe from their lies, from the wicked who stalk us with lies, From the wicked who collect honors For their wonderful lies.

june 30

Psalm 13:1
"A Prayer for Help" from David (GNB)

The chapter of Psalm 13 from The Message Bible is on July 5.

KJV: *[The psalmist is asking the Lord when he will be safe.]* How long wilt thou forget me, O LORD? For ever? How long wilt thou hide they face from me?

NISV: *[The psalmist is asking the Lord when he will be safe.]* How long, O LORD? Will you forget me forever? How long will you hide your face from me?

GNB: *[The psalmist is asking the Lord when he will be safe.]* How much longer will you forget me, LORD? Forever? How much longer will you hide yourself from me?

TMB: *[The psalmist is asking the Lord when he will be safe.]* Long enough, God—you've ignored me long enough. I've looked at the back of your head long enough. Long enough.

David always relied on the Lord to keep him safe from his enemies. We need patience to wait for the Lord, because we have the same assurance that the Lord is here for us.

july 1

Psalm 13:2
"A Prayer for Help" (GNB)

KJV: *[The psalmist is asking the Lord when he will be safe.]* How long shall I take counsel in my soul, having sorrow in my heart daily? How long shall mine enemy be exalted over me?

NISV: *[The psalmist is asking the Lord when he will be safe.]* How long must I wrestle with my thoughts and every day have sorrow in my heart?

GNB: *[The psalmist is asking the Lord when he will be safe.]* How long must I endure trouble? How long will sorrow fill my heart day and night? How long will my enemies triumph over me?

TMB: *[The psalmist is asking the Lord when he will be safe.]* I've carried this ton of trouble, lived with a stomach full of pain. Long enough my arrogant enemies have looked down their noses at me.

When waiting for an answer to prayer, we encounter many challenges and what we think are hardships. The answer does not come when we want it to come. As was said before, God's ways are not our ways, and God's timing is not our timing. Lord, give us the hope and strength to wait patiently for Your answer.

july 2

Psalm 13:3
"A Prayer for Help" from David (GNB)

KJV: *[The psalmist is asking the Lord when he will be safe.]* Consider and hear me, O LORD my God: lighten mine eyes, lest I sleep the sleep of death;

NISV: *[The psalmist is asking the Lord when he will be safe.]* Look on me and answer, O LORD my God. Give light to my eyes, or I will sleep in death;

GNB: *[The psalmist is asking the Lord when he will be safe.]* Look at me, O LORD my God, and answer me. Restore my strength; don't let me die.

TMB: *[The psalmist is asking the Lord when he will be safe.]* Take a good look at me, God, my God; I want to look life in the eye…

As we ask for guidance each day, help us to see things Your way. Help us to learn what we need to know before You take us to the next level of understanding. Thank You for being patient with us. Thank You for showing us the way to find You through prayer and studying Your word.

To find help to study the Bible go to http://bible.christianity. com. There are many references in this web site to help you.

july 3

Psalm 13:4
"A Prayer for Help" from David (GNB)

KJV: *[The psalmist is asking the Lord when he will be safe.]* Lest mine enemy say, I have prevailed against him: and those that trouble me rejoice when I am moved.

NISV: *[The psalmist is asking the Lord when he will be safe.]* My enemy will say, "I have overcome him, and my foes will rejoice when I fall.

GNB: *[The psalmist is asking the Lord when he will be safe.]* Don't let my enemies say, "We have defeated him." Don't let them gloat over my downfall.

TMB: *[The psalmist is asking the Lord when he will be safe.]*…So no enemy can get the best of me or laugh when I fall on my face.

Please protect us from those who would do us harm. Thank You for giving us the assurance that You will be with us even when we fail. We know You will pick us up and help us to go on to complete Your work.

july 4

Psalm 13:5
"A Prayer for Help" from David (GNB)

KJV: *[The psalmist is asking the Lord when he will be safe.]*…But I have trusted in thy mercy; my heart shall rejoice in thy salvation.

NISV: *[The psalmist is asking the Lord when he will be safe.]*…But I trust in your unfailing love; my heart rejoices in your salvation.

GNB: *[The psalmist is asking the Lord when he will be safe.]*…I rely on your constant love; I will be glad, because you will rescue me.

TMB: *[The psalmist is asking the Lord when he will be safe.]*…I've thrown myself headlong into your arms—I'm celebrating your rescue.

Thank You, Lord, for sending Your Son to give us everlasting life and Your love. We praise and thank You for all You do for us.

Ignite your spirit today. Choose your destiny by focusing on the Lord.

july 5

Psalm 13:6
"A Prayer for Help" from David (GNB)

KJV: I will sing unto the LORD, because he hath dealt bountifully with me.

NISV: I will sing to the LORD, for he has been good to me.

GNB: I will sing to you, O LORD, because you have been good to me.

TMB: I'm singing at the top of my lungs, I'm so full of answered prayers.

David has struggled so long waiting for the Lord to rescue him, he is really joyful in his praise to the Lord when he is finally safe.

God wants us to be thankful and express our love to Him in prayer and songs. When we praise the Lord with our singing, it lifts our spirits and floods our soul with love and peace. Thank You, Lord, for all our answered prayers.

The song "Great Is Thy Faithfulness" *part of it says,* "Great is thy faithfulness O God my father. There is no shadow of turning with Thee. Thou changest not, Thy compassions, they fail not, As Thou hast been Thou forever wilt be…All I have needed Thy hand hath provided, 'Great is Thy faithfulness,' Lord, unto me!" *This song tells the whole story of God's love for us.* Words by T.O. Chisholm Music by William M. Runyan.

We have read a verse each day from June 30-July 5, here is the chapter from Psalm 13 from The Message Bible. It gives us a better understanding of the whole chapter:

Psalm 13

Long enough, God—you've ignored me long enough. I've looked at the back of your head long enough. Long enough. I've carried this ton of trouble, lived with a stomach full of pain. Long enough my arrogant enemies have looked down their noses at me. Take a good look at me, God, my God; I want to look life in the eye, So no enemy can get the best of me or laugh when I fall on my face. I've thrown myself headlong into your arms—I'm celebrating your rescue. I'm singing at the top of my lungs, I'm so full of answered prayers.

july 6

Psalm 14:1
"The Wickedness of Men" (GNB)

KJV: *[The psalmist is talking about the deceitful people in his land.]* The fool hath said in his heart, There is no God. They are corrupt, they have done abominable works, there is none that doeth good.

NISV: *[The psalmist is talking about the deceitful people in his land.]* The fool says in his heart, "There is no God." They are corrupt, their deeds are vile; there is no one who does good.

GNB: *[The psalmist is talking about the deceitful people in his land.]* Fools say to themselves, "There is no God!" They are all corrupt, and they have done terrible things; there is no one who does what is right.

TMB: *[The psalmist is talking about the deceitful people in his land.]* Bilious and bloated, they gas, "God is gone." Their words are poison gas, fouling the air; they poison Rivers and skies; thistles are their cash crop.

Whenever there are black-outs for a long period of time, people take advantage of the situation. They loot stores and homes when they think no one is looking. What were they thinking? Obviously they weren't thinking. How could they be so depraved as to take advantage of times when people are so vulnerable. God was watching, and those "unknown" individuals will not walk away unscathed. We have the assurance that the things man can't take care of, God will. He has the final say on everything.

july 7

Psalm 14:2
"The Wickedness of Men" (GNB)

KJV: The LORD looked down from heaven upon the children of men, to see if there were any that did understand, and seek God.

NISV: The LORD looks down from heaven on the sons of men to see if there are any who understand, any who seek God.

GNB: The LORD looks down from heaven at mankind to see if there are any who are wise, any who worship him.

TMB: God sticks his head out of heaven, He looks around. He's looking for someone not stupid—one man, even, God-expectant, just one God-ready woman.

Does it always take an emergency to get our attention? We need to help those around us understand that God is here for us all the time. He is with us every day, emergency or not. He can be your closest, dearest friend.

july 8

Psalm 14: 3
"The Wickedness of Men" (GNB)

KJV: *[The psalmist is talking about the deceitful people in his land.]* They are all gone aside, they are all together become filthy; there is none that doeth good, no, not one.

NISV: *[The psalmist is talking about the deceitful people in his land.]* All have turned aside, they have together become corrupt; there is no one whose good not even one.

GNB: *[The psalmist is talking about the deceitful people in his land.]* But they have all gone wrong; they are all equally bad. Not one of them does what is right, not a single one.

TMB: *[The psalmist is talking about the deceitful people in his land.]* He comes up empty. A string of zeros. Useless, Unshepherded Sheep, taking turns pretending to be Shepherd. The ninety and nine follow their fellow.

If Jesus would come back to earth today, I think He would find more followers than in any other century. However, we still have a lot to do to reach others that have not accepted Christ. The other night on television on the FOX network, Randy Travis was asked if he was a country singer or a gospel singer. He really didn't answer that, but he said, "I went through some rough times, then I found Jesus Christ as my Savior. I sing gospel songs because of what they mean to me."

If you were asked what you believe about Jesus, what would you say?

july 9

Psalm 14:4
"The Wickedness of Men" (GNB)

KJV: *[The psalmist is talking about the deceitful people in his land.]* Have all the workers of iniquity no knowledge? Who eat up my people as they eat bread, and call not upon the LORD.

NISV: *[The psalmist is talking about the deceitful people in his land.]* Will evildoers never learn-those who devour my people as men eat bread and who do not call on the LORD?

GNB: *[The psalmist is talking about the deceitful people in his land.]* "Don't they know?" asks the LORD. "Are all these evildoers ignorant? They live by robbing my people, and they never pray to me."

TMB: *[The psalmist is talking about the deceitful people in his land.]* Don't they know they can't get away with this—Treating people like a fast-food meal over which they're too busy to pray?

The "cool swinging" executives who have been scheming and taking advantage of others are being surprised with jail time and fines. Perhaps others are learning a lesson that white-collar crime doesn't pay.

july 10

Psalm 14:5
"The Wickedness of Men" (GNB)

KJV: *[The psalmist is talking about the deceitful people in his land.]* There were they in great fear: for God is in the generation of the righteous.

NISV: *[The psalmist is talking about the deceitful people in his land.]* There they are, overwhelmed with dread, for God is present in the company of the righteous.

GNB: *[The psalmist is talking about the deceitful people in his land.]* But then they will be terrified, for God is with those who obey him.

TMB: *[The psalmist is talking about the deceitful people in his land.]* Night is coming for them and nightmares, for God takes the side of victims.

Can you imagine the fear and despair that men and women feel when they are sent to prison. Help us to know how to help those behind prison walls. Also, show us how to help those that are heading for trouble. Lord, help us to be honest and follow Your guidance.

Ignite your spirit each day. Choose your destiny by focusing on the Lord and discover His love.

Have you ever helped or visited anyone in prison?

july 11

Psalm 14:6
"The Wickedness of Men" (GNB)

KJV: *[The psalmist is talking about the deceitful people in his land.]* Ye have shamed the counsel of the poor, because the LORD is his refuge.

NISV: *[The psalmist is talking about the deceitful people in his land.]* You evildoers frustrate the plans of the poor, but the LORD is their refuge.

GNB: *[The psalmist is talking about the deceitful people in his land.]* Evildoers frustrate the plans of the humble man, but the LORD is his protection.

TMB: *[The psalmist is talking about the deceitful people in his land.]* Do you think you can mess with the dreams of the poor? You can't for God makes their dreams come true.

We visited Managua, Nicaragua, many years ago on a church mission. The jobless rate was 80 percent. The people who we met there were very poor in materials things, but they were so rich in their love of Jesus. They were dedicated to their church and to helping each other. Their smiles, worship, and happiness brightened every day. They also attended church every day. They taught us and gave us more in love and kindness than we could ever give them in possessions. The poor have a special place in God's heart. Their reward will be great in heaven.

july 12

Psalm 14:7
"The Wickedness of Men" (GNB)

KJV: Oh that the salvation of Israel were come out of Zion! When the LORD bringeth back the captivity of his people, Jacob shall rejoice, and Israel shall be glad.

NISV: Oh, that salvation for Israel would come out of Zion! When the LORD restores the fortunes of his people, let Jacob rejoice and Israel be glad!

GNB: How I pray that victory will come to Israel from Zion. How happy the people of Israel will be when the LORD makes them prosperous again!

TMB: Is there anyone around to save Israel? Yes, God is around; God turns life around. Turned-around Jacob skips rope, turned-around Israel sings laughter.

The focus of the dialogue of the daily readings has been about how the scriptures apply to our daily lives. But God's "chosen" people are the focus of Psalm 14. The country of Israel and its' people are in another gigantic vacuum. What is going to happen there is known only to God. Is it the end of time for this world as we know it? Will Jesus come back to earth soon, in our time?

Help us, Lord, to be ready and to be acceptable to You.

july 13

Psalm 15:1
What God requires of us. (GNB)

Are we good enough to enter the presence of God in His church?

KJV: LORD, who shall abide in thy tabernacle? Who shall dwell in thy holy hill?

NISV: LORD, who may dwell in your sanctuary? Who may live on your holy hill?

GNB: LORD, who may enter your Temple? Who may worship on Zion, your sacred hill?

TMB: God, who gets invited to dinner at your place? How do we get on your guest list?

Jesus wants you to be a part of His family and to live with Him in His heavenly home. It doesn't matter who you are or what you have done. You cannot earn your way by your works or money. Jesus did the work for us when He died on the cross. Many people cannot accept the simplicity of the commitment to become a child of God. All you do is ask God for forgiveness of your sins of the past; He already paid your debt.

july 14

Psalm 15:2
Can we ever measure up to God's expectations?

KJV: *[God honors the people]*...He that walketh uprightly; and worketh righteousness, and speaketh the truth in his heart.

NISV: *[God honors the people.]*...He whose walk is blameless and who does what is righteous; who speaks the truth from his heart.

GNB: *[God honors the people.]*...A person who obeys God in everything and always does what is right, whose words are true and sincere...

TMB: *[God honors the people.]*..."Walk straight, act right, tell the truth."

The laws from the book of Psalms in the Old Testament were for God's people when He first put them on earth. They didn't live up to His expectations. Adam and Eve were human and disobeyed God, which destroyed the perfect union between God and people. Because we are not perfect, He sent His Son and laid the burden of our sins upon Jesus. We cannot measure up to God's expectations. By confessing our sins and asking Jesus to come in and take over our life, we can learn what He wants us to do; to follow Him. We are saved by the love and grace of God our Father.

Ignite your spirit today. Choose your destiny. Ask Jesus to come into your heart.

july 15

Psalm 15:3
Can we do all the right things to please the Lord?

KJV: *[This is the way the Lord would like us to honor Him.]...He that backbiteth not with his tongue, nor doeth evil to his neighbour, nor taketh up a reproach against his neighbour.*

NISV: *[This is the way the Lord would like us to honor Him.]...and has no slander on his tongue, who does his neighbor no wrong and casts no slur on his fellowman,*

GNB: *[This is the way the Lord would like us to honor Him.]...and who does not slander others. He does no wrong to his friends and does not spread rumors about his neighbors.*

TMB: *[This is the way the Lord would like us to honor Him.]...Don't hurt your friend, don't blame your neighbor;*

Even though we should not hurt people by what we say and do, it is our human nature to do what we please and not be perfect. When we do things we know we shouldn't do, we know God will forgive us if when we ask. God will give us wisdom and power to treat others better. God doesn't expect us to be perfect. He just wants us to do our best.

Are there some people you should treat better?

july 16

Psalm 15:4
What God requires from us. (GNB)

KJV: *[This is the way the Lord would like us to honor Him.]*...In whose eyes a vile person is contemned; but he honoureth them that fear the LORD, He that sweareth to his own hurt, and changeth not.

NISV: *[This is the way the Lord would like us to honor Him.]*...Who despises a vile man but honors those who fear the LORD, who keeps his oath even when it hurts,

GNB: *[This is the way the Lord would like us to honor Him.]*...He despises those whom God rejects, but honors those who obey the LORD. He always does what he promises, no matter how much it may cost.

TMB: *[This is the way the Lord would like us to honor Him.]*...despise the despicable. "Keep your word even when it costs you, make an honest living..."

Help us, Lord, to be better people. Help us to listen to Your teachings and follow Your word. Help us to be strong and responsible to those who depend on us.

july 17

Psalm 15:5
What does God expect us to do in everyday life?

KJV: *[This is the way the Lord would like us to honor Him.]*...He that putteth not out his money to usury, nor taketh reward against the innocent. He that doeth these things shall never be moved.

NISV: *[This is the way the Lord would like us to honor Him.]*...who lends his money without usury and does not accept a bribe against the innocent. He who does these things will never be shaken.

GNB: *[This is the way the Lord would like us to honor Him.]*...He makes loans without charging interest and cannot be bribed to testify against the innocent. Whoever does these things will always be secure.

TMB: *[This is the way the Lord would like us to honor Him.]*...never take a bribe. You'll never get blacklisted if you live like this."

God wants us to help those in need by not charging them high interest. Help the needy to get on with their lives even though it may cost you something. God wants to invite all of us to dine at His heavenly table and worship Him in His holy temple. He wants our adoration and praise. God wants to know how much we love Him. We can show God these things by our attitude and how we treat others.

july 18

Psalm 16:1
"A Prayer of Confidence" (GNB)

The chapter of Psalm 16 from The Message Bible is on July 28.

KJV: Preserve me, O God: for in thee do I put my trust.

NISV: Keep me safe, O God, for in you I take refuge.

GNB: Protect me, O God; I trust in you for safety.

TMB: Keep me safe, O God. I've run for dear life to you.

Putting your trust in the Lord will give you long-lasting peace.

july 19

Psalm 16:2
Who is the Lord of your life?

KJV: O my soul, thou hast said unto the LORD. Thou art my LORD: my goodness extendeth not to thee.

NISV: I said to the LORD, "You are my LORD; apart from you I have no good thing."

GNB: I say to the LORD, "You are my LORD; all the good things I have come from you."

TMB: I say to God, "Be my LORD!" Without you, nothing makes sense.

Do you try to run your own show? Have you tried letting God run it for you? He will straighten out your problems in ways you cannot believe. Turn your life over to Him today.

Ignite your spirit each day. Choose your destiny by focusing on the Lord, and discover His love, joy, hope, and peace.

july 20

Psalm 16:3
What does God think about us?

KJV: *[The Lord delights in those who obey Him.]*...But to the saints that are in the earth, and to the excellent, in whom is all my delight.

NISV: *[The Lord delights in those who obey Him.]*...As for the saints who are in the land, they are the glorious ones in whom is all my delight.

GNB: *[The Lord delights in those who obey Him.]*...How excellent are the LORD's faithful people! My greatest pleasure is to be with them.

TMB: *[The Lord delights in those who obey Him.]*...And these God-chosen lives all around—what splendid friends they make!

How do we become God's saints? If we listen and do His work, He will glorify us and reward us in heaven. Can we live a perfect life? No! That is why He sent His Son to save us and will continually forgive our sins.

july 21

Psalm 16:4
Why shouldn't we seek after other gods?

KJV: *[The psalmist tells God how he will honor Him.]...* Their sorrows shall be multiplied that hasten after another god: their drink offerings of blood will I not offer, not take up their names into my lips.

NISV: *[The psalmist tells God how he will honor Him.]...* The sorrows of those will increase who run after other gods. I will not pour out their libations of blood or take up their names on my lips.

GNB: *[The psalmist tells God how he will honor Him.]...* Those who rush to other gods bring many troubles on themselves. I will not take part in their sacrifices; I will not worship their gods.

TMB: *[The psalmist tells God how he will honor Him.]...* Don't just go shopping for a god. Gods are not for sale. I swear I'll never treat god-names like brand-names.

God is a jealous God. He wants us to worship Him and Him alone. What can gods of other cultures possibly do for their people? They have no ears, eyes, or mouths. They cannot hear or answer anyone's prayer. Try relying on the real true God. God and you can't go wrong. What is there to lose? You will gain everything, peace within your heart and soul that no one can take away.

july 22

Psalm 16:5
If you give all you have to God, what will you get in return?

KJV: *[The psalmist tells God how he will honor Him.]*...The LORD is the portion of mine inheritance and of my cup: thou maintainest my lot.

NISV: *[The psalmist tells God how he will honor Him.]*... LORD, you have assigned me my portion and my cup; you have made my lot secure.

GNB: *[The psalmist tells God how he will honor Him.]*...You LORD, are all I have, and you give me all I need: my future is in your hands.

TMB: *[The psalmist tells God how he will honor Him.]*...My choice is you, God, first and only, And now I find I'm your choice!

The Lord has given us everything that we have; everything on this earth really belongs to Him. When we give back to God what is His, He will bless us. Think of all you have been given. We owe our lives and all we have to the creator of the universe.

Ignite your spirit each day. Focus on the Lord. He is our hope.

july 23

Psalm 16:6
What is the most precious thing God has given you?

KJV: *[The psalmist tells God how he will honor Him.]*...The lines are fallen unto me in pleasant places; yea, I have a goodly heritage.

NISV: *[The psalmist tells God how he will honor Him.]*...The boundary lines have fallen for me in pleasant places; surely I have a delightful inheritance.

GNB: *[The psalmist tells God how he will honor Him.]*...How wonderful are your gifts to me; how good they are!

TMB: *[The psalmist tells God how he will honor Him.]*...You set me up with a house and yard. And then you made me your heir!

We are the children of God. He will bless us. Put Him in control of your children, finances, and whatever else is important in your life. You will see how good life can be. Trust in the Lord, let him be Lord over all things.

july 24

Psalm 16:7
Do we give thanks for all the wisdom
God gives us?

KJV: *[The psalmist tells God how he will honor Him.]*...I will bless the Lord, who hath given me counsel: my reins also instruct me in the night seasons.

NISV: *[The psalmist tells God how he will honor Him.]*...I will praise the Lord, who counsels me, even at night my heart instructs me.

GNB: *[The psalmist tells God how he will honor Him.]*...I praise the Lord, because he guides me, and in the night my conscience warns me.

TMB: *[The psalmist tells God how he will honor Him.]*...The wise counsel God gives when I'm awake is confirmed by my sleeping heart.

Many things are revealed to us even in our sleep. Lord, help us to be quiet, patient, and to listen when You speak. Teach us Your ways and give us the wisdom to be the witnesses You want us to be. Let us see the miracles You have for us.

july 25

Psalm 16:8
Where can you find God?

KJV: *[The psalmist tells God how he will honor Him.]*...I have set the LORD always before me: because he is at my right hand, I shall not be moved.

NISV: *[The psalmist tells God how he will honor Him.]*...I have set the LORD always before me. Because he is at my right hand, I will not be shaken.

GNB: *[The psalmist tells God how he will honor Him.]*...I am always aware of the LORD's presence; he is near, and nothing can shake me.

TMB: *[The psalmist tells God how he will honor Him.]*...Day and night I'll stick with God; I've got a good thing going and I'm not letting go.

God is with us 24/7. Friends may come and go, but God is always right where you need Him. Call to Him in all situations. He is waiting for us to depend and trust in Him.

Ignite your spirit each day. Choose your destiny by focusing on the Lord.

july 26

Psalm 16:9
What makes you happy?

KJV: *[The psalmist tells God how he will honor Him.]*... Therefore my heart is glad, and my glory rejoiceth: my flesh also shall rest in hope.

NISV: *[The psalmist tells God how he will honor Him.]*... There my heart is glad and my tongue rejoices; my body also will rest secure...

GNB: *[The psalmist tells God how he will honor Him.]*...And so I am thankful and glad, and I feel completely secure...

TMB: *[The psalmist tells God how he will honor Him.]*...I'm happy from the inside out, and from the outside in, I'm firmly formed.

Are you constantly changing friends? With whom do you hang out? Do your parents approve of the group you hang with? Do you think God approves of your group? Do you feel joy and security that the plan for your life is working? God will give you the confidence that will make your life complete. He will give you peace and joy when you let Him be in charge. Ask Jesus to forgive you of your sin and come into your heart and life today. He wants to be your best friend.

The song "Happy Am I" is a chorus that sticks with you all day. It says:

"Happy am I Jesus loves me. He took my sin and He

set me free." (author unknown) *Think back to when you were a child and the first time you sang "Jesus Loves Me." As you grow older and hear that song sung by others, what kind of feelings come back to you? Do you think Jesus loves you the same way He did when you were a child? Do you love Him the same way you loved Him then?*

Oh Lord, we long for the feelings and innocence of being children. Help us to come to You again that way with a new beginning to learn about You.

Write down how you felt about Jesus when you were a child. Write how you feel about Jesus now.

july 27

Psalm 16:10
Do you feel the protection of God around you?

KJV: *[The psalmist tells God how he will honor Him.]*...For thou wilt not leave my soul in hell; neither wilt thou suffer thine Holy One to see corruption.

NISV: *[The psalmist tells God how he will honor Him.]*...because you will not abandon me to the grave, nor will you let your Holy One see decay.

GNB: *[The psalmist tells God how he will honor Him.]*...because you protect me from the power of death; and the one you love you will not abandon to the world of the dead.

TMB: *[The psalmist tells God how he will honor Him.]*... You canceled my ticket to hell—that's not my destination!

Ask the Lord for His protection and love. He promises in the Bible to save us from our enemies and to take us to heaven to live with Him.

Thank You for the victory You have given us over death and the grave. Thank You, Lord, for giving Your Son on the cross to save us from our sins.

july 28

Psalm 16:11
What does God promise us?

KJV: *[The psalmist tells God how he will honor Him.]*... Thou wilt shew me the path of life: in thy presence is fullness of joy; at thy right hand there are pleasures for evermore.

NISV: *[The psalmist tells God how he will honor Him.]*...You have made known to me the path of life; you will fill me with joy in your presence, with eternal pleasures at your right hand.

GNB: *[The psalmist tells God how he will honor Him.]*...You will show me the path that leads to life; your presence fills me with joy and brings me pleasure forever.

TMB: *[The psalmist tells God how he will honor Him.]*...Now you've got my feet on the life path, all radiant from the shining of your face. Ever since you took my hand, I'm on the right way.

Let the Lord be the savior of your heart and soul. Only He can give the joy and peace you desperately need.

We have read a verse each day from July 18 to 29; below is the chapter of Psalm 16 from The Message Bible.

Keep me safe, O God. I've run for dear life to you. I say to God, "Be my Lord!" Without you, nothing makes sense. And these God-chosen lives all around—what splendid friends they make! Don't just go shopping for a god. Gods are not for sale. I swear I'll never treat god-names like brand-names. My choice is you, God, first and only, And now I find I'm your choice! You set me up with a house and yard. And then you made me your heir! The wise counsel God gives when I'm awake is confirmed by my sleeping heart. Day and night I'll stick with God; I've got a good thing going and I'm not letting go. I'm happy from the inside out, and from the outside in, I'm firmly formed. You canceled my ticket to hell—that's not my destination! Now you've got my feet on the life path, all radiant from the shining of your face. Ever since you took my hand, I'm on the right way.

july 29

Psalm 18:1
"David's Song of Victory" (GNB)

KJV: I will love thee, O Lord, my strength.

NISV: I love you, O Lord, my strength.

GNB: How I love you, Lord! You are my defender.

TMB: I love you, God—you make me strong.

God, thank you for loving us.
    Write what you think about God today.

july 30

Psalm 18:2
"David's Song of Victory" (GNB)

How David perceived God.

KJV: The LORD is my rock, and my fortress, and my deliverer; my God, my strength, in whom I will trust; my buckler, and the horn of my salvation, and my high tower.

NISV: The LORD is my rock, my fortress and my deliverer; my God is my rock, in whom I take refuge. He is my shield and the horn of my salvation, my stronghold.

GNB: The LORD is my protector he is my strong fortress. My God is my protection, and with him I am safe. He protects me like a shield; he defends me and keeps me safe.

TMB: God is bedrock under my feet. The castle in which I live, my rescuing knight. My God—the high crag where I run for dear life, hiding behind the boulders, safe in the granite hideout.

An old familiar hymn that we still sing is called "The Solid Rock." *The chorus says,* "On Christ, the solid Rock, I stand—All other ground is sinking sand." "The Solid Rock" words by Edward Mote; music by William B. Bradbury; "Living Hymns" Encore Publications, Inc.

Even though these scriptures are from Psalms, they relate to the New Testament and Jesus, the rock of our salvation. We can depend on that solid foundation.

Thank You for giving us the rock Christ Jesus, and taking away the sinking sand.

july 31

Psalm 18:3
"David's Song of Victory" (GNB)

How David perceived God.

- KJV: I will call upon the LORD, who is worthy to be praised; so shall I be saved from mine enemies.
- NISV: I call to the LORD, who is worthy of praise, and I am saved from my enemies.
- GNB: I call to the LORD, and he saves me from my enemies. Praise the LORD!
- TMB: I sing to God, the Praise-Lofty, and find myself safe and saved.

When we praise the Lord, we honor Him and give Him our thanks. He is our hope and peace.

august 1

Psalm 18:4
"David's Song of Victory" (GNB)

How David perceived God.

KJV: The sorrows of death compass me, and the floods of ungodly men made me afraid.

NISV: The cords of death entangled me; the torrents of destruction overwhelmed me.

GNB: The danger of death was all around me; the waves of destruction rolled over me.

TMB: The hangman's noose was tight at my throat; devil waters rushed over me.

Are you afraid of dying? When you face death, you can know that God will be waiting with open arms. Ask Him to forgive you of your sins and accept Him into your heart. Jesus has taken care of everything by dying on the cross for all of us. We have the free will and choice to accept this gift of His Son. Choose your destiny.

What are your feelings about death? (Read *Life After Death* by Billy Graham)

august 2

Psalm 18:5
"David's Song of Victory" (GNB)

How David perceived God.

KJV: The sorrows of hell compassed me about: the snares of death prevented me…

NISV: The cords of the grave coiled around me; the snares of death confronted me…

GNB: The danger of death was around me, and the grave set its trap for me.

TMB: Hell's ropes cinched me tight; death traps barred every exit.

In all his trials, David believed the Lord would deliver him, and He did. Do you have the assurance that God will do this for you? Trust in the Lord, believe in Him, and He will deliver you.

august 3

Psalm 18:6
"David's Song of Victory" (GNB)

How David perceived God.

- KJV: In my distress I called upon the LORD, and cried unto my God: he heard my voice out of his temple, and my cry came before him, even unto his ears.

- NISV: In my distress I called to the LORD; I cried to my God for help. From his temple he heard my voice; my cry came before him, into his ears.

- GNB: In my trouble I called to the LORD; I called to my God for help. In his temple he heard my voice; he listened to my cry for help.

- TMB: A hostile world! I call to God, I cry to God to help me. From his palace he hears my call; my cry brings me right into his presence—a private audience!

Don't wait until you have an emergency to ask God to take care of you. God is by your side at all times. God is waiting for you to ask for His help. Trust Him; He will take care of you.

How do you handle the stress in your life?

august 4

Psalm 18:7
"David's Song of Victory" (GNB)

How David perceived God.

KJV: Then the earth shook and trembled; the foundations also of the hills moved and were shaken because he was wroth.

NISV: The earth trembled and quaked and the foundation of the mountains shook; they trembled because he was angry.

GNB: Then the earth trembled and shook: the foundations of the mountains rocked and quivered, because God was angry.

TMB: Earth wobbles and lurches, high mountains shake like leaves; quake like aspen leaves because of his rage.

God's anger can move mountains; think of how much He can do for us. We need to ask Him for His help and believe He will answer our prayers. We limit what the Lord will do for us because we do not ask Him to help us.

august 5

Psalm 18:8
"David's Song of Victory" (GNB)

How David perceived God.

KJV: There went up a smoke out of his nostrils, and fire out of his mouth devoured: coals were kindled by it.

NISV: Smoke rose from his nostrils; consuming fire came from his mouth, burning coals blazed out of it.

GNB: Smoke poured out of his nostrils, a consuming flame and burning coals from his mouth.

TMB: His nostrils flare, bellowing smoke; his mouth spits fire. Tongues of fire dart in and out, he lowers the sky.

The wrath of the Lord is mighty. Being a child of God gives us the assurance that we will not feel His wrath but His grace.

august 6

Psalm 18:9
"David's Song of Victory" (GNB)

How David perceived God.

KJV: He bowed the heavens also, and came down: and darkness was under his feet.

NISV: He parted the heavens and came down; dark clouds were under his feet.

GNB: He tore the sky open and came down with a dark cloud under his feet.

TMB: He steps down; under his feet an abyss opens up.

In David's picture of Jesus coming down to earth, we see God's power and grandeur. All on earth will worship Him.

august 7

Psalm 18:10
"David's Song of Victory" (GNB)

How David perceived God.

KJV: And he rode upon a cherub, and did fly: yea, he did fly upon the wings of the wind.

NISV: He mounted the cherubim and flew and soared on the wings of the wind.

GNB: He flew swiftly on his winged creature; he traveled on the wings of the wind.

TMB: He's riding a winged creature, swift on wind-wings.

Write what you think Jesus will look like when He comes to earth to rescue us and take us to our heavenly home.

august 8

Psalm 18:11
"David's Song of Victory" (GNB)

How David perceived God.

KJV: He made darkness his secret place; his pavilion round about him *were* dark waters and thick clouds of the skies.

NISV: He made darkness his covering his canopy around him—the dark rain clouds of the sky.

GNB: He covered himself with darkness; thick clouds, full of water, surrounded him.

TMB: Now he's wrapped himself in a trench coat of black-cloud darkness.

God comes to save us where we are. We can't save ourselves or earn His salvation. All we need to do is pray, and He will rescue us and keep us safe. We have to rely on His power and not our own.

If you don't have a prayer box, get a box and cut a hole in the top. Decorate the box if you would like. Write down your prayers and put them in the box. Check every week or so to see how your prayers are being answered.

august 9

Psalm 18:12
"David's Song of Victory" (GNB)

How David perceived God.

KJV: At the brightness that was before him his thick clouds passed, hail stones and coals of fire.

NISV: Out of the brightness of his presence clouds advanced with hailstones and bolts of lightning.

GNB: Hailstones and flashes of fire came from the lightning before him and broke through the dark clouds.

TMB: But his cloud-brightness bursts through, spraying hailstones and fireballs.

The sight of God coming back to earth will be more breathtaking than any fireworks display we have ever seen. The song "Jesus Is Coming Again" says, "O what a wonderful day that will be—Jesus is coming again!" ("Jesus Is Coming Again" words, Thomas Kelly; music, William H. Monk.)

Are you looking forward to Jesus coming back to earth?

august 10

Psalm 18:13
"David's Song of Victory" (GNB)

How David perceived God.

KJV: The LORD also thundered in the heavens, and the Highest gave his voice; hail stones and coals of fire.

NISV: The LORD thundered from the heaven; the voice of the Most High resounded.

GNB: Then the LORD thundered from the sky; and the voice of the Most High was heard.

TMB: Then God thundered out of heaven; the High God gave a great shout, spraying hailstones and fireballs.

The display God will create at His coming will make all people of the earth aware of His mighty power. Read Revelation for all the details.

august 11

Psalm 18:14
"David's Song of Victory" (GNB)

How David perceived God.

KJV: Yea, he sent out his arrows, and scattered them; and he shot out lightnings, and discomfited them.

NISV: He shot his arrows and scattered his enemies, great bolts of lightning and routed them.

GNB: He shot his arrows and scattered his enemies; with flashes of lightning he sent them running.

TMB: God shoots his arrows—pandemonium! He hurls his lightnings—a rout!

God will root out all who are hiding from Him. There is nowhere to hide. God is everywhere. Read Revelation, the last book of the Bible.

august 12

Psalm 18:15
"David's Song of Victory" (GNB)

How David perceived God.

KJV: Then the channels of waters were seen, and the foundations of the world were discovered at thy rebuke, O LORD, at the blast of the breath of thy nostrils.

NISV: The valleys of the sea were exposed and the foundations of the earth laid bare at your rebuke, O LORD at the blast of breath from your nostrils.

GNB: The floor of the ocean was laid bare, and the foundations of the earth were uncovered, when you rebuked your enemies, LORD and roared at them in anger.

TMB: The secret sources of ocean are exposed, the hidden depths of earth lie uncovered. The moment you roar in protest, let loose your hurricane anger...

God has made all that is in the earth. He controls the sea and the sky. He allows you to think you are in control and have no need for Him. In the end, God will show everyone how He is in control of everything.

august 13

Psalm 18:16
"David's Song of Victory" (GNB)

How David perceived God.

KJV: He sent from above, he took me, he drew me out of many waters.

NISV: He reached down from on high and took hold of me; he drew me out of deep waters.

GNB: The LORD reached down from above and took hold of me; he pulled me out of the deep waters.

TMB: But me he caught—reached all the way from sky to sea; he pulled me out…

The Lord will save you no matter who you are or where you are. He always knows who you are and where you are.

The song "The Solid Rock" *says,* "My hope is built on nothing less than Jesus' blood and righteousness; I dare not trust the sweetest frame But wholly lean on Jesus' name. On Christ the solid rock I stand, all other ground is sinking sand." *Christ Jesus is the only one that can keep you from falling into the paths of sin.* ("The Solid Rock" words and music by Wm. B. Bradbury.

Jesus is waiting for your cry for help and offers forgiveness to all that call on His name.

august 14

Psalm 18:17
"David's Song of Victory" (GNB)

How David perceived God.

- KJV: He delivered me from my strong enemy, and from them which hated me: for they were too strong for me.
- NISV: He rescued me from my powerful enemy, from my foes who were to strong for me.
- GNB: He rescued me from my powerful enemies and from all those who hate me—they were too strong for me.
- TMB: *[God rescued me]* of that ocean of hate, that enemy chaos, the void in which I was drowning.

Have you ever felt like you were drowning? God will reach down and pull you up, up to His level and save you. Your enemies cannot defeat what you turn over to God.

august 15

Psalm 18:18
"David's Song of Victory" (GNB)

How David perceived God.

KJV: They prevented me in the day of my calamity: but the LORD was my stay.

NISV: They confronted me in the day of my disaster, but the LORD was my support.

GNB: When I was in trouble, they attacked me, but the LORD protected me.

TMB: They hit me when I was down, but God stuck by me.

It doesn't matter who is after you or who may want to attack you. God is with you and will help you. Ask Jesus to come into your heart and take away your sin. Turn your life and problems over to Him. What do you have to lose? He will be closer than your best friend and will be with you in every way.

august 16

Psalm 18:19
"David's Song of Victory" (GNB)

How David perceived God.

KJV: He brought me forth also into a large place; he delivered me, because he delighted in me.

NISV: He brought me out into a spacious place; he rescued me because he delighted in me.

GNB: He helped me out of danger; he saved me because he was pleased with me.

TMB: He stood me up on a wide-open field; I stood there saved—surprised to be loved!

God will take care of you because He loves you. He gave His only Son for your sins. Talk to God today; it will be the best day of your life.

august 17

Psalm 18:20
"David's Song of Victory" (GNB)

How David perceived God.

KJV: The LORD rewarded me according to my righteousness; according to the cleanness of my hands hath he recompensed me.

NISV: The LORD has dealt with me according to my righteousness; according to the cleanness of my hands has he rewarded me

GNB: The LORD rewards me because I do what is right; he blesses me because I am innocent.

TMB: God made my life complete when I placed all the pieces before him.

The Lord forgives and forgets all our past sin. He will make everything right in your life.

Trust Him to turn your worst night into the best day. Why not have His assurance that He will love you and keep you safe? He is waiting for you with open arms. All it takes is a prayer. God will perform miracles in your life.

Do you feel forgiven of your sins?

august 18

Psalm 18:21
"David's Song of Victory" (GNB)

How David pleased God.

KJV: For I have kept the ways of the LORD, and have not wickedly departed from my God.

NISV: For I have kept the ways of the LORD; I have not done evil by turning from my God.

GNB: I have obeyed the law of the LORD; I have not turned away from my God.

TMB: When I got my act together, he gave me a fresh start.

When we start over with God, He will help us follow Him. Through our prayers and studying the Bible, He will show us what He expects from us.

august 19

Psalm 18:22
"David's Song of Victory" (GNB)

How David pleased God.

KJV: For all his judgments were before me, and I did not put away his statutes from me.

NISV: All his laws are before me; I have not turned away from his decrees.

GNB: I have observed all his laws; I have not disobeyed his commands.

TMB: Now I'm alert to God's ways. I don't take God for granted.

Every day we make mistakes and terrible decisions. When the Lord claims us as one of His children, we know that no matter how bad we mess up, He will forgive us. Obeying and serving God will give us peace in our heart. God will give us strength and grace to get through every day.

august 20

Psalm 18:23
"David's Song of Victory" (GNB)

How David pleased God.

KJV: I was upright before him, and I kept myself from mine iniquity.

NISV: I have been blameless before him and have kept myself from sin.

GNB: He knows that I am faultless, that I have kept myself from doing wrong.

TMB: Every day I review the ways he works; I try not to miss a trick.

Let God guide your every step. This way you can be sure you are pleasing the Lord. We can't be perfect because only God is perfect. Ask for forgiveness when you make a mistake and God will make everything right.

august 21

Psalm 18:24
"David's Song of Victory" (GNB)

How David pleased God.

KJV: Therefore hath the Lord recompensed me according to my righteousness, according to the cleanness of my hands in his eyesight.

NISV: The Lord has rewarded me according to my righteousness, according to the cleanness of my hands in his sight.

GNB: And so he rewards me because I do what is right, because he knows that I am innocent.

TMB: I feel put back together, and I'm watching my step.

When we follow the Lord, He will reward us. Our reward is not on this earth but in heaven.

What kind of a reward do you think you will receive from the Lord? You have free will to change your life; do you like who you are now? Pray about what you want to do with the rest of your life.

august 22

Psalm 18:25
"David's Song of Victory" (GNB)

How David pleased God.

KJV: With the merciful thou wilt shew thyself merciful: with an upright man thou wilt shew thyself upright.

NISV: To the faithful you show yourself faithful, to the blameless you show yourself blameless.

GNB: O LORD, you are faithful to those who are faithful to you; completely good to those who are perfect.

TMB: God rewrote the text of my life when I opened the book of my heart to his eyes.

If someone watched how you lived for a few days and had to give a report about you, what kind of a report do you think they would turn in? What do the people around you think about you? God watches us every day every hour. Do you ever think about what He says in your book of life?

Write about what you observe in the life of one of your friends. Are they a witness to you? Are they the kind of people you want to have as an influence on your life? Compare it to what you see in your own life. What kind of an influence do you have on your friends?

august 23

Psalm 18:26
"David's Song of Victory" (GNB)

David talks about God.

KJV: With the pure thou wilt shew thyself pure: and with the froward thou wilt shew thyself froward.

NISV: ...to the pure you show yourself pure, but to the crooked you show yourself shrewd.

GNB: You are pure to those who are pure, but hostile to those who are wicked.

TMB: The good people taste your goodness. The whole people taste your health. The true people taste your truth. The bad ones can't figure you out.

Unless you know God and have a relationship with Him, you can't know what He has for your life. People that do not have a personal relationship with God cannot understand Him because He deals with them as if they are unworthy children. We need to teach others how to find God's grace and forgiveness so they too can become part of God's family.

august 24

Psalm 18:27
"David's Song of `Victory" (GNB)

David talks about God.

KJV: For thou wilt save the afflicted people; but wilt bring down high looks.

NISV: You save the humble but bring low those whose eyes are haughty.

GNB: You save those who are humble, but you humble those who are proud.

TMB: You take the side of the down-and-out, But the stuck-up you take down a peg.

Lord, help us to let You take care of the people that treat us badly. We know You will deal with those who think they run the show. Help us to be good examples to people around us.

august 25

Psalm 18:28
"David's Song of Victory" (GNB)

David talks about God.

KJV: For thou wilt light my candle: the LORD my God will enlighten my darkness.

NISV: You, O LORD, keep my lamp burning; my God turns my darkness into light.

GNB: O LORD, you give me light; you dispel my darkness.

TMB: Suddenly, God you floodlight my life; I'm blazing with glory, God's glory!

Do others see God's light in us? If God can't count on us to be His light, how will He reach the people around us?

Make a list of things you could do to reach your friends and family.

august 26

Psalm 18:29
"David's Song of Victory" (GNB)

David talks about God.

KJV: For by thee I have run through a troop; and by my God have I leaped over a wall.

NISV: With your help I can advance against a troop; with my God I can scale a wall.

GNB: You give me strength to attack my enemies and power to overcome their defenses.

TMB: I smash the bands of marauders, I vault the highest fences.

How much do you trust the Lord? Do you believe He can help you do things you never thought you could do? If we trust Him completely, the rewards are great. Call upon His name, not just when you are in trouble, but let Him run your whole life every minute of every day.

august 27

Psalm 18:30
"David's Song of Victory" (GNB)

David talks about God.

KJV: As for God his way is perfect: the word of the LORD is tried: he is a buckler to all those that trust in him.

NISV: As for God, his way is perfect; the word of the LORD is flawless. He is a shield for all who take refuge in him.

GNB: This God—how perfect are his deeds! How dependable his words! He is like a shield for all who seek his protection.

TMB: What a God! His road stretches straight and smooth. Every God-direction is road-tested. Everyone who runs toward him Makes it.

God tells us the truth. We need to learn to listen to His word. He will keep us strong. There is no one like God. Accept His promises and grace.

august 28

Psalm 18:31
"David's Song of Victory" (GNB)

David talks about God.

- KJV: For who is God save the LORD? Or who is a rock save our God?
- NISV: For who is God besides the LORD? And who is the Rock except our God?
- GNB: The LORD alone is God; God alone is our defense.
- TMB: Is there any god like *God*? Are we not at bedrock?

David believed with all his heart, mind and soul that God would deliver him. Just think of what God did for David. We who believe and trust in God are just as special to God. Believe in God for what you need. He will not let you down.

Do you feel forgiven of your sins?

august 29

Psalm 18:32
"David's Song of Victory" (GNB)

David talks about God.

KJV: It is God that girdeth me with strength, and maketh my way perfect.

NISV: It is God who arms me with strength and makes my way perfect.

GNB: He is the God who makes me strong, who makes my pathway safe.

TMB: Is not this the God who armed me, then aimed me in the right direction?

David was alone. God was his only protection. David believed God would deliver him and He did. God was definitely with David when he killed the giant.

What do you want God to deliver you from? Make a list of things that God will help you do.

august 30

Psalm 18:33
"David's Song of Victory" (GNB)

David talks about God.

KJV: He maketh my feet like hinds' feet, and setteth me upon my high places.

NISV: He makes my feet like the feet of a deer; he enables me to stand on the heights.

GNB: He makes me sure-footed as a deer; he keeps me safe on the mountains.

TMB: Now I run like a deer; I'm king of the mountain.

With God running your life, you can conquer any problem. He will swiftly take care of you and show you how to be the best person possible.

august 31

Psalm 18:34
"David's Song of Victory" (GNB)

David talks about God.

KJV: He teacheth my hands to war, so that a bow of steel is broken by mine arms.

NISV: He trains my hands for battle; my arms can bend a bow of bronze.

GNB: He trains me for battle, so that I can use the strongest bow.

TMB: He shows me how to fight; I can bend a bronze bow!

God made David so strong he could defeat any enemy. We can know that God will help us take care of anyone that tries to harm us.

Look back at the past month's verses. Has anything changed in your life because of what you learned or did?

Write down the changes that have taken place or the changes you are thinking of making. Let the Lord speak to you; let Him make a difference.

september 1

Psalm 18:35
"David's Song of Victory" (GNB)

David talks about God.

KJV: Thou hast also given me the shield of thy salvation: and thy right Hand hath holden me up, and thy gentleness hath made me great.

NISV: You give me your shield of victory, and your right hand sustains me; you stoop down to make me great.

GNB: O Lord, you protect me and save me; your care has made me great, and your power has kept me safe.

TMB: You protect me with salvation-armor; you hold me up with a firm hand, caress me with your gentle ways.

Can you think of something special the Lord has done for you? Let us thank the Lord for all He does for us.

september 2

Proverbs 3:5
Benefits of the Lord's Wisdom

KJV: Trust in the Lord with all thine heart; and lean not unto thine own understanding.

NISV: Trust in the Lord with all your heart and lean not on your own understanding:

GNB: Trust in the Lord with all your heart. Never rely on what you think you know.

TMB: Trust God from the bottom of your heart; don't try to figure out everything on your own.

Where have you put your trust?

september 3

Proverbs 3:6
Benefits of the Lord's Wisdom

KJV: In All thy ways acknowledge him, and he shall direct they paths.

NISV: In all your ways acknowledge him, and he will make your path's straight.

GNB: Remember the LORD in everything you do, and he will show you the right way.

TMB: Listen for God's voice in everything you do, everywhere you go, he's the one who will keep you on track.

Do you allow the Lord to work through you?

Try praying your way through the day. Jesus is the only friend that is always with you. You don't have to dial Him on the phone and leave a message or wait until He finishes His work to talk to you. He is waiting to hear and answer your requests all day and night.

The song "What a Friend We Have in Jesus" *tells us how He cares for us.* "What a friend we have in Jesus, All our sins and griefs to bear! What a privilege to carry everything to God in prayer!…We should never be discouraged, Take it to the Lord in prayer. Can we find a friend so faithful, Who will all our sorrows share? Jesus knows our every weakness, Take it to the Lord in prayer." "What a Friend We Have in Jesus" words by Joseph Scriven; music byCharles C. Converse.

How could you find a better friend?

september 4

Proverbs 3:12
Benefits of the Lord's Wisdom

KJV: For whom the LORD loveth he correcteth; even as a father the son *in whom* he delighteth.

NISV: [Listen children,]…the LORD disciplines those he loves, as a father the son he delights in.

GNB: The Father corrects those he loves. As a father corrects a son of whom he is proud.

TMB: It's the child he loves that God corrects; a father's delight is behind all this.

When we do things we know we shouldn't do, we wonder who is watching. The Lord tries to teach us by correcting us. Parents do the same. If you don't want the punishment, think before you act.

september 5

Proverbs 3:15
Benefits of the Lord's Wisdom

KJV: She [wisdom] is more precious than rubies: and all the things thou canst desire are not to be compared unto her.

NISV: She [wisdom] is more precious than rubies; nothing you desire can compare with her.

GNB: Wisdom offers you long life, as well as wealth and honor.

TMB: She's [wisdom] worth far more than money in the bank; her friendship is better than a big salary.

We find wisdom by studying God's word. What you have in your mind will always be with you. Take time to memorize scriptures from the Bible. The wisdom you learn from scriptures will comfort you and bring you guidance.

september 6

Proverbs 3:21-23
Benefits of the Lord's Wisdom

KJV: [Children keep wisdom and understanding]…let them not depart from thine eyes: keep sound wisdom and discretion: [22] So shall they be life unto thy soul, and grace to thy neck. [23] Then shalt thou walk in thy way safely, and thy foot shall not stumble.

NISV: My [children]…preserve sound judgment and discernment, do not let them out of your sight; [22] They will be life for you, an ornament to grace your neck. [23] Then you will go on your way in safety, and your foot will not stumble;

GNB: Son, hold on to your wisdom and insight. Never let them get away from you. [22] They will provide you with life-a pleasant and happy life. [23] You can go safely on your way and never even stumble.

TMB: Dear friend, guard Clear Thinking and Common Sense with your life; don't for a minute lose sight of them. [22] They'll keep your soul alive and well, they'll keep you fit and attractive. [23] You'll travel safely, you'll neither tire or trip.

Do you understand the Bible? There are many ways to learn more about the Bible. Find a Bible study class to attend or look at this web site: www.lifesgreatestquestion.com/way-home.

september 7

Proverbs 4:1
Benefits of the Lord's Wisdom

KJV: Hear, ye children, the instruction of a father, and attend to know understanding.

NISV: Listen, my sons, to a father's instructions; pay attention and gain understanding.

GNB: Sons, listen to what your father teaches you. Pay attention, and you will have understanding.

TMB: Listen, friends, to some fatherly advice; sit up and take notice so you'll know how to live.

You need to know God before you ask for His help. If you are a child of God, He will hear your call for help. Give God a chance to show you a better way of life. You can have a relationship with God by asking Him to forgive your sins and come into your life.

september 8

Proverbs 4:6
Benefits of the Lord's Wisdom

KJV: Forsake her not, [wisdom] and she shall preserve thee: love, and she shall keep thee.

NISV: Do not forsake wisdom, and she will protect you; love her, and she will watch over you.

GNB: Do not abandon wisdom, and she will protect you; love her, and she will keep you safe.

TMB: Above all and before all, do this: Get Wisdom! Write this at the top of your list: Get understanding!

Who is your mentor? Whose wisdom do you rely on? Are you happy with what you know about Jesus?

september 9

Ecclesiastes 3:1
A time for all things.

KJV: To every thing there is a season, and a time to every purpose under the heaven:

NISV: There is a time for everything, and a season for every activity under heaven:

GNB: Everything that happens in this world happens at the time God chooses.

TMB: There's an opportune time to do things, a right time for everything on the earth.

Is this the right time to rededicate yourself to what God wants you to do?

september 10

Ecclesiastes 12:13
The sum total of our life.

KJV: …Fear God, and keep his commandments: for this is the whole duty of man.

NISV: …Fear God and keep his commandments, for this is the whole duty of man

GNB: …Have reverence for God, and obey his commands, because this is all that man was created for.

TMB: …Fear God. Do what he tells you.

The Purpose Driven Life *tells us that God put us on earth to praise and serve Him.* Read *The Purpose Driven Life,* by Rick Warren.

How do you fear and praise God?

september 11

John 14:1
The way to find our Father.

KJV: "Let not your heart be troubled; ye believe in God; believe also in me."

NISV: "Do not let your hearts be troubled, Trust in God trust also in me.

GNB: "Do not be worried and upset." Jesus told them. "Believe in God and believe also in me."

TMB: Don't let this throw you. You trust God, don't you? Trust me.

God will give you peace. All we need to do is accept the gift He has given us, His Son, Jesus, as our Savior.

september 12

John 14: 2
The way to find our Father.

- KJV: "In my Father's house are many mansions: if it were not so, I would have told you. I go to prepare a place for you."
- NISV: "In my Father's house are many rooms; if it were not so, I would have told you. I am going there to prepare a place for you."
- GNB: "There are many rooms in my Father's house, and I am going to prepare a place for you. I would not tell you this if it were not so."
- TMB: "There is plenty of room for you in my Father's home. If that weren't so, would I have told you that I'm on my way to get your room ready."

The home we live in on this earth may not be a mansion, but Jesus says He is building a mansion for us in heaven. That mansion will be the happiest home we will ever experience, with His love to surround us.

Do you want heaven to be your home?

september 13

John 14:3
The way to find our Father.

KJV: *[Jesus said]*…"And if I go and prepare a place for you, I will come again, and receive you unto myself; that where I am, there ye may be also."

NISV: *[Jesus said]*…"And if I go and prepare a place for you, I will come back and take you to be with me that you also may be where I am"

GNB: *[Jesus said]*…"And after I go and prepare a place for you, I will come back and take you to myself, so that you will be where I am."

TMB: *[Jesus said]*…"I'll come back and get you so you can live where I live."

Thank You, Lord, for Your promises.

september 14

John 14:6
The way to find our Father.

KJV: Jesus saith unto him, I am the way, the truth, and the life: no man cometh unto the Father, but by me.

NISV: Jesus answered, "I am the way and the truth and the life. No one comes to the Father except through me."

GNB: Jesus answered him, "I am the way, the truth, and the life; no one goes to the Father except by me.

TMB: Jesus said, "I am the Road, also the Truth, also the Life. No one gets to the Father apart from me."

Have you been seeking happiness and still feel empty? Life in Jesus will fill your emptiness. Return to trusting Him today or start from the beginning. Just ask for His forgiveness and He will meet you where you are.

september 15

Proverbs 4:26
Benefits of the Lord's Wisdom

KJV: Ponder the path of thy feet, and let all thy ways be established.

NISV: Make level paths for your feet and take only ways that are firm.

GNB: Plan carefully what you do, and whatever you do will turn out right.

TMB: Watch your step, and the road will stretch out smooth before you.

Others are watching and they wonder who you really are. Where do your feet take you? Are you being honest about your sincerity to live for God?

september 16

Psalms 31:7
"A Prayer of Trust in God"

KJV: I will be glad and rejoice in thy mercy: for thou hast considered my trouble; thou hast known my soul in adversities;

NISV: I will be glad and rejoice in your love, for you saw my affliction and knew the anguish of my soul.

GNB: I will be glad and rejoice because of your constant love. You see my suffering; you know my trouble.

TMB: I am leaping and singing in the circle of your love; you saw my pain, you disarmed my tormentors.

The Lord knows all our trouble before we tell Him. He watches us day by day and knows our needs. His mercy covers every prayer we whisper to Him.

What do you think about God? Do you trust Him as your Savior? Do you think He can deliver you from any situation?

september 17

Psalm 19:1
"God's Glory in Creation" (GNB)

How the sun, moon, stars, and planets display God's glory.

KJV: The heavens declare the glory of God; and the firmament sheweth his handywork.

NISV: The heavens declare the glory of God; the skies proclaim the work of his hands.

GNB: How clearly the sky reveals God's glory! How plainly it shows what he has done!

TMB: God's glory is on tour in the skies, God-craft on exhibit across the horizon.

By looking at the stars, planets, and physical world around us, how could anyone doubt Intelligent Design? Our God who takes care of us each day gave us this world. He made all the wonderful things of creation. The beautiful sunsets reveal to us a touch of His glorious reflection.

Earlier in this book, I mentioned a new Creation Museum in Petersburg, Kentucky, a little town about twenty miles southeast of the Cincinnati airport. It has wonderful exhibits for children and adults. The time line starts at creation and finishes with the present day. Here is the website if you want to check it out: www.CreationMuseum.org.

september 18

Psalm 19:2
"God's Glory in Creation" (GNB)

How the sun, moon, stars, and planets display God's glory.

KJV: Day unto day uttereth speech, and night unto night sheweth knowledge.

NISV: Day after day they pour forth speech; night after night they display knowledge.

GNB: Each day announces it to the following day; each night repeats it to the next.

TMB: Madame Day holds classes every morning, Professor Night lectures each evening.

Dear Lord, every day we thank You for letting the sun come up. Each new day gives us another chance to worship You. We thank You for the night and the rest we need.

september 19

Psalm 19:3
"God's Glory in Creation" (GNB)

How the sun, moon, stars, and planets display God's glory.

- KJV: There is no speech nor language, where their voice is not heard.
- NISV: There is no speech or language where their voice is not heard.
- GNB: No speech or words are used; no sound is heard.
- TMB: Their words aren't heard; their voices aren't recorded.

We thank You, God, for all the wonders of Your universe. Thank You for the magnificent creation You have made for us to enjoy.

september 20

Psalm 19:4
"God's Glory in Creation" (GNB)

How the sun, moon, stars, and planets display God's glory.

KJV: Their line is gone out through all the earth, and their words to the end of the world. In them hath he set a tabernacle for the sun.

NISV: Their voice goes out into all the earth, their words to the ends of the world. In the heavens he has pitched a tent for the sun.

GNB: …yet their voice goes out to all the world and is heard to the ends of the earth. God made a home in the sky for the sun.

TMB: But their silence fills the earth: unspoken truth is spoken everywhere. God makes a huge dome for the sun—a superdome!

The breathtaking beauty of the sun coming up over the horizon declares You have given us another day to worship. The glory of creation shows us how perfect You made the world. Help us treat Your world with respect.

september 21

Psalm 19:5
"God's Glory in Creation" (GNB)

How the sun, moon, stars, and planets display God's glory.

KJV: *[The sun comes up each morning]*…Which is as a bridegroom coming out of his chamber, and rejoiceth as a strong man to run a race.

NISV: *[The sun comes up each morning]*…which is like a bridegroom coming forth from his pavillion, like a champion rejoicing to run his course.

GNB: *[The sun]*…it comes out in the morning like a happy bridegroom, like an athlete eager to run a race.

TMB: The morning sun's a new husband leaping from his honeymoon bed, The daybreaking sun an athlete racing to the tape.

The sun wakes us to a new day and the awesome possibilities of our walk with God. Our journey with Him makes everything possible.

september 22

Psalm 19:6
"God's Glory in Creation" (GNB)

How the sun, moon, stars, and planets display God's glory.

KJV: His going forth is from the end of the heaven, and his circuit unto the ends of it: and there is nothing hid from the heat thereof.

NISV: It rises at one end of the heavens and makes its circuit to the other; nothing is hidden from its heat.

GNB: It starts at one end of the sky and goes across to the other. Nothing can hide from its heat.

TMB: That's how God's Word vaults across the skies from sunrise to sunset, Melting ice, scorching deserts, warming hearts to faith.

My husband's favorite song "This Is My Father's World" *tells us* "This is my Father's world. All nature sings. And round me rings, The music of the sphere's.…The birds their carols raise, The morning light, and lily white, Declare their Maker's praise…He shines in all that's fair; In the rustling grass I hear Him pass, He speaks to me everywhere. This is my Father's world: The battle is not done; Jesus who died shall be satisfied, And earth and heaven be one."

"This Is My Father's World" words by Maltbie D. Babcock; music by Franklin L. Sheppard.

We thank You, O Lord, for the wonderful mysteries of Your earth.

september 23

Psalm 19:7
"The Law of the Lord" (GNB)

KJV: The law of the LORD is perfect, converting the soul: the testimony of the LORD is sure, making wise the simple.

NISV: The law of the LORD is perfect reviving the soul. The statutes of the LORD are trustworthy making wise the simple.

GNB: The law of the LORD is perfect; it gives new strength. The commands of the LORD are trustworthy, giving wisdom to those who lack it.

TMB: The revelation of God is whole and pulls our lives together.

As we study the Bible, God will teach us what He wants us to learn.

This web site has many Bible studies available: http://bible.christianity.com. *Click on Bible in A Year.*

september 24

Psalm 19:8
"The Law of the Lord" (GNB)

KJV: The statutes of the LORD are right, rejoicing the heart: the commandment of the LORD is pure, enlightening the eyes.

NISV: The precepts of the LORD are right, giving joy to the heart. The commands of the LORD are radiant, giving light to the eyes.

GNB: The laws of the LORD are right, and those who obey them are happy. The commands of the LORD are just and give understanding to the mind.

TMB: The signposts of God are clear and point out the right road. The life-maps of God are right, showing the way to joy. The directions of God are plain and easy on the eyes.

Many of the laws given in the books of Leviticus and Deuteronomy are still used in our culture today. Read through these books of the Bible. It will amaze you how the old laws are incorporated into our everyday lives. The Lord gives us truth. How much easier our lives would be if we learned to obey His word.

september 25

Psalm 19:9
"The Law of the Lord" (GNB)

KJV: The fear of the Lord is clean, enduring forever: the judgments of the Lord are true and righteous altogether.

NISV: The fear of the Lord is pure, enduring forever. The ordinances of the Lord are sure and altogether righteous.

GNB: The worship of the Lord is good; it will continue forever. The judgments of the Lord are just: they are always fair.

TMB: God's reputation is twenty-four-carat gold, with a lifetime guarantee. The decisions of God are accurate down to the nth degree.

God does not give wrong directions. He will guide every step.

september 26

Psalm 19:10
"The Law of the Lord" (GNB)

KJV: *["The ways of the Lord are."]*…More to be desired are they than gold, yea, than much fine gold: sweeter also than honey and the honeycomb.

NISV: *["The ways of the Lord."]*…They are more precious than gold, than much pure gold: they are sweeter than honey, than honey from the comb.

GNB: *["The ways of the Lord."]*…They are more desirable than the finest gold; they are sweeter than the purest honey.

TMB: God's Word is better than a diamond, better than a diamond set between emeralds. You'll like it better than strawberries in spring, better than red, ripe strawberries.

The gold and diamonds of the law that God gives us cannot be stolen from us. They are the pillars from which we build our lives. His word, the Bible, is more precious than any jewel. We can trust Him to be right in all things.

Write down and memorize a new scripture today.

september 27

Psalm 19:11
"The Law of the Lord" (GNB)

KJV: *[The psalmist is talking about the ways of the Lord.]* Moreover by them is thy servant warned: and in keeping of them there is great reward.

NISV: *[The psalmist is talking about the ways of the Lord.]* By them is your servant warned; in keeping them there is great reward.

GNB: *[The psalmist is talking about the ways of the Lord.]* They give knowledge to me, your servant; I am rewarded for obeying them.

TMB: *[The psalmist is talking about the ways of the Lord.]* There's more: God's Word warns us of danger and directs us to hidden treasure.

Our reward is in the daily peace He gives us. In keeping the laws "under His grace" from the New Testament, our reward is to spend eternity with Him.

september 28

Psalm 19:12
"The Law of the Lord" (GNB)

KJV: *[The psalmist is talking about the ways of the Lord.]* Who can understand his errors: cleanse thou me from secret faults.

NISV: *[The psalmist is talking about the ways of the Lord.]* Who can discern his errors? Forgive my hidden faults.

GNB: *[The psalmist is talking about the ways of the Lord.]* No one can see his own errors; deliver me, LORD, from hidden faults!

TMB: *[The psalmist is talking about the ways of the Lord.]* Otherwise how will we find our way? Or know when we play the fool? Clean the slate, God so we can start the day fresh!

Lord, help us to admit our mistakes and help us to correct them. Help us to live a life pleasing to You.

september 29

Psalm 19:13
"The Law of the Lord" (GNB)

KJV: *[The psalmist is talking about the ways of the Lord.]* Keep back thy servant also from presumptuous sins; Let them not have dominion over me: then shall I be upright, and I shall be innocent from the great transgression.

NISV: *[The psalmist is talking about the ways of the Lord.]* Keep your servant also from willful sins; may they not rule over me. Then will I be blameless, innocent of great transgression.

GNB: *[The psalmist is talking about the ways of the Lord.]* Keep me safe, also, from willful sins; don't let them rule over me. Then I shall be perfect and free from the evil of sin.

TMB: *[The psalmist is talking about the ways of the Lord.]* Keep me from stupid sins, from thinking I can take over your work. Then I can start this day sun-washed, scrubbed clean of the grime of sin.

We have so much to learn. Help us to listen when you speak. Teach us how You want us to live.

september 30

Psalm 19:14
"The Law of the Lord" (GNB)

KJV: *[The psalmist is talking about the ways of the Lord.]* Let the words of my mouth, and the meditation of my heart, be acceptable in thy sight, O Lord my strength, and my redeemer.

NISV: *[The psalmist is talking about the ways of the Lord.]* May the words of my mouth and meditation of my heart be pleasing in your sight O Lord, my Rock and my Redeemer.

GNB: *[The psalmist is talking about the ways of the Lord.]* May my words and my thoughts be acceptable to you, O Lord, my refuge and my redeemer!

TMB: *[The psalmist is talking about the ways of the Lord.]* These are the words in my mouth; these are what I chew on and pray. Accept them when I place them on the morning altar, O God, my Altar-Rock, God, Priest-of-My-Altar.

We hear this verse used at the end of many church services. If the words and thoughts from our hearts were made known, would they we be acceptable in God's sight? If we turn our lives over to God, how differently our hearts and minds would perceive the world. God would give us peace of mind and help make our lives worth living.

This is the chapter of Psalm 19 from the Kings James

Version of the Bible quoted on dates September 16 to 30. I hope you enjoy reading the chapter in its entirety:
"Glory in God's Creation" and the "Law of the Lord"

The heavens declare the glory of God; and the firmament sheweth his handywork. Day unto day uttereth speech, and night unto night sheweth knowledge. There is no speech nor language, where their voice is not heard. Their line is gone out through all the earth, and their words to the end of the world. In them hath he set a tabernacle for the sun. Which is as a bridegroom coming out of his chamber, and rejoiceth as a strong man to run a race. His going forth is from the end of the heaven, and his circuit unto the ends of it: and there is nothing hid from the heat thereof. The law of the Lord is perfect, converting the soul: the testimony of the Lord is sure, making wise the simple. The statutes of the Lord are right, rejoicing the heart: the commandment of the Lord is pure, enlightening the eyes. The fear of the Lord is clean, enduring for ever: the judgments of the Lord are true and righteous altogether. More to be desired are they than gold, yea, than much fine gold: sweeter also than honey and the honeycomb. Moreover by them is thy servant warned: and in keeping of them there is great reward. Who can understand his errors: cleanse thou me from secret faults. Keep back thy servant also from presumptuous sins; Let them not have dominion over me: then shall I be upright, and I shall be innocent from the great transgression. Let the words of my mouth, and the meditation of my heart, be acceptable in thy sight, O Lord my strength, and my redeemer.

october 1

Deuteronomy 32:39
Are there any gods greater than our
Father in heaven?

KJV: See now that I, even I, am he, and there is no god like me: I kill, and I make alive; I wound and I heal: neither is there any that can deliver out of my hand.

NISV: See now that I myself am He! There is no god besides me. I put to death and I bring to life, I have wounded and I will heal, and no one can deliver out of my hand.

GNB: I, and I alone am God; no other god is real. I kill and I give life, I wound and I heal, and no one can oppose what I do.

TMB: "Do you see it now? Do you see that I'm the one? Do you see that there's no other god beside me? I bring death and I give life, I wound and I heal—there is no getting away from or around me!"

My parents sang on a radio program for many years. The theme song of the program was "God Of Our Fathers" *This song tells about the majesty of our God.* "God of our Fathers, whose almighty hand Leads forth in beauty all the starry band Of shining worlds in splendor through the skies, Our grateful songs before Thy throne arise."

Words by Daniel C. Roberts (written in 1876) Music by George W. Warren, (written in 1892)

We do not need to call on many different gods. Our God is the only true God. He will answer all our prayers.

october 2

Matthew 6:33-34
What do you worry about? Does worry keep you awake at night and bother you all day?

KJV: But seek ye first the kingdom of God, and his righteousness; and all these things shall be added unto you. ³⁴ Take therefore no thought for the morrow: for the morrow shall take thought for the things of itself. Sufficient unto the day is the evil thereof.

NISV: But seek first his kingdom and his righteousness, and all these things will be given to you as well. ³⁴ Therefore, do not worry about tomorrow, for tomorrow will worry about itself. Each day has enough trouble of its own.

GNB: Instead be concerned above everything else with the Kingdom of God and with what he requires of you, and he will provide you with all these other things. ³⁴ So do not worry about tomorrow: it will have enough worries of it its own. There is no need to add to the troubles each day brings.

TMB: "Give your entire attention to what God is doing right now, don't get worked up about what may or may not happen tomorrow. God will help you deal with whatever hard things come up when the time comes."

Ask the Lord to forgive your sins. Romans 10:13 says, "Everyone who calls out to the Lord for help will be saved" (GNB). Turn everything over to the Lord, and He will give you peace.

october 3

Daniel 6:22
Do you believe your God can save you
from the "lions" around you?

King Darius was forced to throw Daniel into the lion's den, where Daniel spent the night. Early in the morning the king, being very worried about Daniel, went to the lion's pit and called to Daniel, "Daniel, servant of the living God! Was the God you serve able to save you from the lions?" Daniel answered:

KJV: My God hath sent his angel, and hath shut the lions mouths, that they have not hurt me: forasmuch as before him innocency was found in me: and also before thee, O king, have I done no hurt.

NISV: "My God sent his angel, and he shut the mouths of the lions. They have not hurt me, because I was found innocent in his sight. Nor have I ever done any wrong before you, O king."

GNB: God sent his angel to shut the mouths of the lions so that they would not hurt me. He did this because he knew that I was innocent and because I have not wronged you, Your Majesty

TMB: "My God sent his angel, who closed the mouths of the lions so that they would not hurt me. I've been found innocent before God and also before you, O king. I've done nothing to harm you."

The king was overjoyed and ordered all his people to worship Daniel's God, the only true God. What will it take to make us believe in God?

Write about your experience with God. If He isn't in your life, now is the time to ask Him to come in.

october 4

Luke 14:13-14
How often do we reach out to those less fortunate then ourselves?

KJV: "But when thou makest a feast, call the poor, the maimed, the lame, the blind: ¹⁴ And thou shalt be blessed; for they cannot recompense thee: for thou shalt be recompensed at the resurrection of the just."

NISV: "But when you give a banquet, invite the poor, the crippled, the lame, the blind, ¹⁴ And you will be blessed. Although they cannot repay you, you will be repaid at the resurrection of the righteous."

GNB: "When you give a feast, invite the poor, the crippled, the lame, and the blind; and you will be blessed, because they are not able to pay you back. God will repay you on the day the good people rise from death."

TMB: "...The next time you put on a dinner, don't just invite your friends and family and rich neighbors, the kind of people who will return the favor. Invite some people who never get invited out, the misfits from the wrong side of the tracks. You'll be—and experience—a blessing. They won't be able to return the favor, but the favor will be returned—oh, how it will be returned—at the resurrection of God's people."

God wants us to remember the poor in spirit and poor in material things. We should help our "neighbors" in as many ways as possible.

october 5

1 Thessalonians 5:16-18
Remember to rejoice and be thankful;
God is listening to all we say.

KJV: Rejoice evermore. ¹⁷ Pray without ceasing. ¹⁸ In every thing give thanks: for this is the will of God in Christ Jesus concerning you.

NISV: Be joyful always, ¹⁷ pray continually; ¹⁸ give thanks in all circumstances, for this is God's will for you in Christ Jesus.

GNB: Be joyful always, ¹⁷ pray at all times, ¹⁸ be thankful in all circumstances. This is what God wants from you in your life in union with Christ Jesus.

TMB: Be cheerful no matter what; pray all the time; thank God no matter what happens. This is the way God wants you who belong to Christ Jesus to live.

It is impossible to be able to pray all the time. But as you go through each day, keep in mind that God's Spirit is with you. We can call upon Him at any time. Praising God in our hearts and remembering what we are thankful for will raise our spirits. What a great way to relieve stress.

If you don't have a prayer box, make one by putting a slit in the top of a box. Decorate the box if you like. Write down your prayer requests on a slip of paper and put them in the box. Check it weekly or monthly and see how your prayers are being answered.

october 6

Psalm 27:1
"A Prayer of Praise" (GNB)

Psalm 27 from The Message Bible is on October 19.

KJV: The Lord is my light and my salvation; whom shall I fear? The Lord is the strength of my life; of whom shall I be afraid?

NISV: The Lord is my light and my salvation-whom shall I fear? The Lord is the stronghold of my life-of whom shall I be afraid?

GNB: The Lord is my light and my salvation; I will fear no one. The Lord protects me from all danger; I will never be afraid.

TMB: Light, space, zest—that's God! So, with him on my side I'm fearless, afraid of no one and nothing.

Let the Lord be your strength and let Him give you power to calm your fear. He will not let you down. Just ask Him to come into your life; He will give you strength.

Who is the Lord of your life? Of whom are you afraid? It might help to put your feelings on paper. Write about your fears.

october 7

Psalm 27:2
"A Prayer of Praise" (GNB)

KJV: *[The psalmist's conversation with God]*...When the wicked, even mine enemies and my foes, came upon me to eat up my flesh, they stumbled and fell.

NISV: *[The psalmist's conversation with God]*...When evil men advance against me to devour my flesh, when my enemies and my foes attack me, they will stumble and fall.

GNB: *[The psalmist's conversation with God]*...When evil men attack me and try to kill me they stumble and fall.

TMB: *[The psalmist's conversation with God]*...When vandal hordes ride down ready to eat me alive, Those bullies and toughs fall flat on their faces.

Help us to accept Your assistance in calming our fears. Remind us to call on Your name even when we are not in need.

october 8

Psalm 27:3
"A Prayer of Praise" (GNB)

KJV: *[The psalmist's conversation with God]*...Though an host should encamp against me, my heart shall not fear: though war should rise against me, in this will I be confident.

NISV: *[The psalmist's conversation with God]*...Though an army besiege me, my heart will not fear; though war break out against me, even then will I be confident.

GNB: *[The psalmist's conversation with God]*...Even if a whole army surrounds me, I will not be afraid; even if enemies attack me, I will still trust God.

TMB: *[The psalmist's conversation with God]*...When besieged, I'm as calm as a baby. When all hell breaks loose, I'm collected and cool.

Keep your mind on God when you are distressed. Teach us to trust You and rely on Your word that says You will never leave us or forsake us.

This is quote from a sermon at the Twin Towers United Methodist Church in Alameda, California: "I have prepared a disaster kit. If we are caught shorthanded and have not prepared for an emergency, we put ourselves in a bad situation. Preparing our hearts and minds for a heavenly kingdom will save us for eternity. What is in your disaster kit?"

The best way to have an emergency disaster kit to take with you everywhere you go is to memorize as much scripture as possible. Start with a short verse. Practice saying it five times a day for a week and writing it at least three times a day. You will be surprised how many verses you can remember. The scripture will be available to you when you need it.

Memorize the 23rd Psalm; it only has six verses. These verses will do wonders in helping you slow down and prioritize your life.

october 9

Psalm 27:4
"A Prayer of Praise" (GNB)

KJV: *[The psalmist's conversation with God]*...One thing have I desired of the LORD, that will I seek after; that I may dwell in the house of the LORD all the days of my life, to behold the beauty of the LORD, and to inquire in his temple.

NISV: *[The psalmist's conversation with God]*...One thing I ask of the LORD, this is what I seek: that I may dwell in the house of the LORD all the days of my life, to gaze upon the beauty of the LORD and to seek him in his temple.

GNB: *[The psalmist's conversation with God]*...I have asked the LORD for one thing; one thing only do I want: to live in the LORD's house all my life, to marvel there at his goodness, and to ask for his guidance.

TMB: *[The psalmist's conversation with God]*...I'm asking God for one thing: To live with him in his house my whole life long. I'll contemplate his beauty; I'll study at his feet.

When we spend eternity with God, we will see the glorious home He has prepared for us. We can worship at His feet and praise Him all day long.

My father sang in a men's quartet. On Sunday night they would sing in the church service. One of my favorite songs was

"Mansion Over the Hilltop." The chorus says, "I got a mansion just over the hilltop in that bright land where we'll never grow old. And some day yonder we'll never more wander and walk the streets that are paved with pure gold." Composers Unknown

october 10

Psalm 27:5
"A Prayer of Praise" (GNB)

KJV: *[The psalmist's conversation with God]*...For in the time of trouble he shall hide me in his pavilion; in the secret of his tabernacle shall he hide me; he shall set me up upon a rock.

NISV: *[The psalmist's conversation with God]*...For in the day of trouble he will keep me safe in his dwelling; he will hide me in the shelter of his tabernacle and set me high upon a rock.

GNB: *[The psalmist's conversation with God]*...In times of trouble he will shelter me; he will keep me safe in his Temple and make me secure on a high rock.

TMB: *[The psalmist's conversation with God]*...That's the only quiet, secure place in a noisy world, The perfect getaway, far from the buzz of traffic.

David seemed to have a lot of enemies. He was chosen by God, to be king and the head of the royal lineage of Israel. David had many problems; Bathsheba, armies chasing him, and other battles he had to fight. But God kept getting him back on track and forgiving him for all the trouble he got into. So, when we look at David's life, it will help us realize that we do have a forgiving God. There are many other people in the Bible that did not live an upstanding, perfect life. God waited for those people to come around and realize they needed Him in their lives.

If you don't know God, call to Him and He will come and find you where you are, just as you are. Let Him help you change your outlook on life and give you joy.

october 11

Psalm 27:6
"A Prayer of Praise" (GNB)

KJV: *[The psalmist's conversation with God]*...And now shall mine head be lifted up above mine enemies round about me: therefore will I offer in his tabernacle sacrifices of joy; I will sing, yea, I will sing praises unto the Lord.

NISV: *[The psalmist's conversation with God]*...Then my head will be exalted above the enemies who surround me; at his tabernacle will I sacrifice with shouts of joy; I will sing and make music to the Lord.

GNB: *[The psalmist's conversation with God]*...So I will triumph over my enemies around me. With shouts of joy I will offer sacrifices in his Temple; I will sing, I will praise the Lord.

TMB: *[The psalmist's conversation with God]*...God holds me head and shoulders above all who try to pull me down. I'm headed for his place to offer anthems that will raise the roof! Already I'm singing God songs, I'm making music to God.

Let us sing praises to the Lord. He knows our trouble. We praise God for all He has done for us.

october 12

Psalm 27:7
"A Prayer of Praise" (GNB)

KJV: *[The psalmist's conversation with God]*…Hear, O LORD, when I cry with my voice: have mercy also upon me, and answer me.

NISV: *[The psalmist's conversation with God]*…Hear my voice when I call, O LORD; be merciful to me and answer me.

GNB: *[The psalmist's conversation with God]*…Hear me, LORD, when I call to you! Be merciful and answer me!

TMB: *[The psalmist's conversation with God]*…Listen, God, I'm calling at the top of my lungs "Be good to me! Answer me!"

God have mercy on us; send us your miracles and blessings.

october 13

Psalm 27:8
"A Prayer of Praise" (GNB)

KJV: *[The psalmist's conversation with God]*...When thou saidst, Seek ye my face; my heart said unto thee, Thy face, Lord, will I seek

NISV: *[The psalmist's conversation with God]*...My heart says of you, "Seek his face!" Your face, Lord, I will seek.

GNB: *[The psalmist's conversation with God]*...When you said, "Come worship me," I answered, "I will come, Lord."

TMB: *[The psalmist's conversation with God]*...When my heart whispered, "Seek God," my whole being replied, "I'm seeking him!"

To seek the face of God, we need to know Him. We get to know God by studying the Bible.

Memorize as much scripture as possible. Pick a short verse and practice saying it five times a day and write it three times a day. You could start memorizing with one of the verses above.

Challenge yourself to choose your destiny by focusing on discovering God's love and peace in your life.

october 14

Psalm 27:9
"A Prayer of Praise" (GNB)

KJV: *[The psalmist's conversation with God]*...Hide not thy face far from me; put not thy servant away in anger: thou hast been my help leave me not, neither forsake me, O God of my salvation.

NISV: *[The psalmist's conversation with God]*...Do not hide your face from me; do not turn your servant away in anger; you have been my helper. Do not reject me or forsake me, O God my Savior.

GNB: *[The psalmist's conversation with God]*...Don't hide yourself from me! Don't be angry with me; don't turn your servant away. You have been my help; don't leave me, don't abandon me, O God, my savior.

TMB: *[The psalmist's conversation with God]*...Don't hide from me now! You've always been right there for me; don't turn your back on me now. Don't throw me out, don't abandon me, you've always kept the door open.

How do you call out to the Lord?
 What answers has He given you?
 Have you thanked Him for being the guide of your life?

october 15

Psalm 27:10
"A Prayer of Praise" (GNB)

KJV: *[The psalmist's conversation with God]*…When my father and my mother forsake me, then the LORD will take me up.

NISV: *[The psalmist's conversation with God]*…Though my father and mother forsake me, the LORD will receive me.

GNB: *[The psalmist's conversation with God]*…My father and mother may abandon me, but the LORD will take care of me.

TMB: *[The psalmist's conversation with God]*…My father and mother walked out and left me, but God took me in.

Some children never know their mother or father. Those who have parents may lose their parents through death. And sometimes we don't get along with our parents. But we have a heavenly Father that is always with us. His love and instruction to us has always been the same—it will not change or fail us. If you have not had a relationship with a father or mother or have lost your parents, God, our heavenly Father, is always on call. He is listening to hear your cry for help. Let Him take your burden and let Him be a father to you. Just pray now and ask Him to forgive you of your sins. He will come into your life and be your father and a true friend.

october 16

Psalm 27:11
"A Prayer of Praise" (GNB)

KJV: *[The psalmist's conversation with God]*...Teach me thy way, O LORD, and lead me in a plain path, because of mine enemies.

NISV: *[The psalmist's conversation with God]*...Teach me your way, O LORD; lead me in a straight path because of my oppressors.

GNB: *[The psalmist's conversation with God]*...Teach me, LORD, what you want me to do, and lead me along a safe path, because I have many enemies.

TMB: *[The psalmist's conversation with God]*...Point me down your highway, God; direct me along a well-lighted street; show my enemies whose side you're on.

David knew the Lord was with Him. Our cry to the Lord will be heard and answered just like David's.

october 17

Psalm 27:12
"A Prayer of Praise" (GNB)

KJV: *[The psalmist's conversation with God]*...Deliver me not over unto the will of mine enemies; for false witnesses are risen up against me, and such as breathe out cruelty.

NISV: *[The psalmist's conversation with God]*...Do not turn me over to the desire of my foes, for false witnesses rise up against me, breathing out violence.

GNB: *[The psalmist's conversation with God]*...Don't abandon me to my enemies, who attack me with lies and threats.

TMB: *[The psalmist's conversation with God]*...Don't throw me to the dogs, those liars who are out to get me, filling the air with their threats.

When anyone says bad things about us, we feel dejected and hurt. Don't even think about taking revenge on them. The people who lie and cheat will be taken care of by God.

Write about how God helped you get over something that was done to you. Did you go to the person and talk about it? Is there something you need to settle now?

october 18

Psalm 27:13
"A Prayer of Praise" (GNB)

KJV: *[The psalmist's conversation with God]*...I had fainted, unless I had believed to see the goodness of the Lord in the land of the living.

NISV: *[The psalmist's conversation with God]*...I am still confident of this: I will see the goodness of the Lord in the land of the living.

GNB: *[The psalmist's conversation with God]*...I know that I will live to see the Lord's goodness in this present life.

TMB: *[The psalmist's conversation with God]*...I'm sure now I'll see God's goodness in the exuberant earth.

Do we look around this cruel world and wonder what will happen to all of us? God is in control! We may not be around to see the end times, but it is God's world and He will take care of all things.

october 19

Psalm 27:14
"A Prayer of Praise" (GNB)

KJV: *[Our instructions from the psalmist.]* Wait on the LORD: be of good courage, and he shall strengthen thine heart: wait, I say, on the LORD.

NISV: *[Our instructions from the psalmist.]* Wait for the LORD; be strong and take heart and wait for the LORD.

GNB: *[Our instructions from the psalmist.]* Trust in the LORD. Have faith, do not despair. Trust in the LORD.

TMB: *[Our instructions from the psalmist.]* Stay with God! Take heart. Don't quit. I'll say it again: Stay with God.

"God is good all the time. All the time God is good." (Author Unknown)

This is the complete chapter from Psalms 27 from The Message Bible. Please enjoy reading it to get a better sense of the psalm.

Light, space, zest—that's God! So, with him on my side I'm fearless, afraid of no one and nothing. When vandal hordes ride down ready to eat me alive, Those bullies and toughs fall flat on their faces. When besieged, I'm calm as a baby. When all hell breaks loose, I'm collected and cool. I'm asking God for one thing: To live with him in his house my whole life long. I'll contemplate his beauty; I'll study at his feet. That's the only quiet, secure place in a noisy world, The perfect getaway, far from the buzz of traffic. God holds me head and shoulders above all who try to pull me down. I'm headed for his place to offer anthems that will raise the roof! Already I'm singing God songs, I'm making music to God. Listen, God, I'm calling at the top of my lungs "Be good to me! Answer me!" When my heart whispered, "Seek God," my whole being replied, "I'm seeking him!" Don't hide from me now! You've always been right there for me; don't turn your back on me now. Don't throw me out, don't abandon me, you've always kept the door open. My father and mother walked out and left me, but God took me in. Point me down your highway, God; direct me along a well-lighted street; show my enemies whose side you're on. Don't throw me to the dogs, those liars who are out to get me, filling the air with their threats. I'm sure now I'll see God's goodness in the exuberant earth. Stay with God! Take heart. Don't quit. I'll say it again: Stay with God.

october 20

Psalm 46:1
"God Is with Us" (GNB)

KJV: God is our refuge and strength, a very present help in trouble.

NISV: God is our refuge and strength, an ever-present help in trouble.

GNB: God is our shelter and strength, always ready to help in times of trouble.

TMB: God is a safe place to hide, ready to help when we need him.

When we are stressed beyond belief, we even forget how to think. But God is always with us. Remember He is waiting to help us with all our needs. Just pray to Him and He will help you. When you don't know what to say when you pray, just ask for His help. He already knows the problem and will help you with the solution.

The 23rd Psalm from the NISV Bible is easy to memorize. Use it for a meditation or a prayer. Memorize a verse each day and you will know it by the end of the week.

1 "The Lord is my shepherd. I shall not want.
2 He makes me lie down in green pastures, he leads me beside quiet waters,
3 He restores my soul. He guides me in paths of righteousness for his name's sake.

4 Even though I walk through the valley of the shadow of death, I will fear no evil, for you are with me.

5 You prepare a table before me in the presence of my enemies. You anoint my head with oil; my cup overflows.

6 Surely goodness and love will follow me all the days of my life, and I will dwell in the house of the Lord forever."

october 21

Psalm 46:2
"God Is with Us" (GNB)

KJV: Therefore will not we fear, though the earth be removed, and though the mountains be carried into the midst of the sea.

NISV: Therefore we will not fear, though the earth give way and the mountains fall into the heart of the sea.

GNB: So we will not be afraid, even if the earth is shaken and mountains fall into the ocean depths.

TMB: We stand fearless at the cliff-edge of doom, courageous in seastorm and earthquake.

The Lord takes care of the earth, mountains, and sea. He cares even more for us, His children. He will calm our fears.

We sing many songs that we can recall in time of need. A part of the chorus of one of those songs is "Are you weary, are you heavy hearted? Tell it to Jesus, Tell it to Jesus, He is a friend that's well known; You've no other such a friend or brother. Tell it to Jesus alone." "Tell It To Jesus" *words by Jeremiah E. Rankin; music by Edmund S. Lorenz.*

Jesus is always ready to listen.

october 22

Psalm 46:3
"God Is with Us" (GNB)

KJV: Though the waters thereof roar and be troubled, though the mountains shake with the swelling thereof. Selah

NISV: Though its water roar and foam and the mountains quake with their surging. Selah

GNB: ...even if the seas roar and rage, and the hills are shaken by the violence.

TMB: Before the rush and roar of oceans, the tremors that shift mountains. (Jacob-wrestling God fights for us, God of the Angel Armies protects us.)

This year we have experienced many natural disasters. Every day we hear people praising God for saving them and their families. We must have a strong and steadfast faith that God is with us and will take care of us. Do you have that kind of faith?

Write about what the Lord means to you.

october 23

Psalm 46:4
"God Is with Us" (GNB)

KJV: There is a river, the streams whereof shall make glad the city of God, the holy place of the tabernacles of the most High.

NISV: There is a river whose streams make glad the city of God, the holy place where the Most High dwells.

GNB: There is a river that brings joy to the city of God, to the sacred house of the Most High.

TMB: River fountains splash joy, cooling God's city, this sacred haunt of the Most High.

The river mentioned above is also mentioned in Revelation 22:1 KJV: "And he shewed me a pure river of water of life, clear as crystal proceeding from the throne of God and of the Lamb." *This is the river that will flow through Jerusalem and give life to everything when Jesus comes back to live on earth. Until that time the living water of the word of Jesus is the everlasting water of the eternal life He gives us.*

october 24

Psalm 46:5
"God Is with Us" (GNB)

KJV: …God is in the midst of her; she shall not be moved: God shall help her, and that right early.

NISV: …God is within her, she will not fall; God will help her at break of day.

GNB: …God is in that city, and it will never be destroyed; at early dawn he will come to its aid.

TMB: …God lives here, the streets are safe. God at your service from crack of dawn.

The city (her) in this verse is Jerusalem. When Jesus walks this earth again, the city of Jerusalem will belong to the believers in Christ. His holy and radiant light will reign forever.

october 25

Psalm 46:6
"God Is with Us" (GNB)

KJV: The heathen raged, the kingdoms were moved: he uttered his voice, the earth melted.

NISV: Nations are in uproar, kingdoms fall: he lifts his voice, the earth melts.

GNB: Nations are terrified, kingdoms are shaken: God thunders, and the earth dissolves.

TMB: Godless nations rant and rave, kings and kingdoms threaten, but Earth does anything he says.

God may allow bad things to happen in this world, but He is still in charge! He will take care of everything in His own time.

october 26

Psalm 46:7
"God Is with Us" (GNB)

- KJV: The LORD of hosts is with us; the God of Jacob is our refuge. Selah.
- NISV: The LORD Almighty is with us; the God of Jacob is our fortress. Selah.
- GNB: The LORD Almighty is with us; the God of Jacob is our refuge.
- TMB: Jacob-wrestling God fights for us. God of the Angel Armies protects us.

God is in charge even though bad things happen! He will take care of everything in His own time. (This is being deliberately repeated. Please think about it.)

october 27

Psalm 46:8
"God Is with Us" (GNB)

KJV: Come, behold the works of the LORD, what desolations he hath made in the earth.

NISV: Come and see the works of the LORD, the desolations he has brought on the earth.

GNB: Come and see what the LORD has done. See what amazing things he has done on earth.

TMB: Attention, all! See the marvels of God! He plants flowers and trees all over the earth.

It doesn't matter what goes on in this world. God is in charge! He will take care of everything in His own time. (This is being repeated. Please think about it.)

october 28

Psalm 46:9
"God Is with Us" (GNB)

KJV: He maketh wars to cease unto the end of the earth; he breaketh the bow, and cutteth the spear in sunder; he burneth the chariot in the fire.

NISV: He makes wars cease to the ends of the earth; he breaks the bow and shatters the spear, he burns the shields with fire.

GNB: He stops wars all over the world, he breaks bows, destroys spears, and sets shields on fire.

TMB: Bans war from pole to pole, breaks all the weapons across his knee.

God is in charge of all things! *He will take care of everything in His own way.*
   (This is being repeated. Please think about it.)

october 29

Psalm 46:10
"God Is with Us" (GNB)

KJV: Be still, and know that I am God: I will be exalted among the heathen, I will be exalted among the earth.

NISV: Be still, and know that I am God; I will be exalted among the nations, I will be exalted in the earth.

GNB: "Stop fighting," he says, "and know that I am God, supreme among the nations, supreme over the world."

TMB: "Step out of the traffic! Take a long loving look at me, your High God above politics, above everything."

God is in charge!

october 30

Psalm 46:11
"God Is with Us" (GNB)

KJV: The LORD of Hosts is with us; the God of Jacob is our refuge. Selah.

NISV: The LORD Almighty is with us; the God of Jacob is our fortress. Selah.

GNB: The LORD Almighty is with us; the God of Jacob is our refuge.

TMB: Jacob-wrestling God fights for us, God of the Angel Armies protects us.

The complete chapter of Psalm 46 as discussed from October 20 to October 30, from The Message Bible:

> God is a safe place to hide, ready to help when we need him. We stand fearless at the cliff-edge of doom, courageous in seastorm and earthquake, before the rush and roar of oceans, the tremors that shift mountains. (Jacob-wrestling God fights for us, God of the Angel Armies protects us.) River fountains splash joy, cooling God's city, this sacred haunt of the Most High. God lives here, the streets are safe. God at your service from crack of dawn. Godless nations rant and rave, kings and kingdoms threaten, but Earth does anything he says. (Jacob-wrestling God fights for us. God of the Angel Armies protects us.) Attention, all! See the marvels

of God! He plants flowers and trees all over the earth. Bans war from pole to pole, breaks all the weapons across his knee. "Step out of the traffic! Take a long loving look at me, your High God above politics, above everything." Jacob-wrestling God fights for us, God of the Angel Armies protects us.

Verse 7 and verse 11 are the same. God repeats very important messages in the Bible. We need to think about what He is saying to us. So I am repeating again: God is in charge! He will take care of everything in His own time.

october 31

Psalm 93:1
"God the King" (GNB)

Psalm 93 from the The Message Bible is on November 4th.

KJV: The LORD reigneth, he is clothed with majesty; the LORD is clothed with strength, wherewith he hath girded himself: the world also is stablished, that it cannot be moved.

NISV: The LORD reigns, he is robed in majesty, the LORD is robed in majesty and is armed with strength. The word is firmly established; it cannot be moved.

GNB: The LORD is king. He is clothed with majesty and strength. The earth is set firmly in place and cannot be moved.

TMB: God is King, robed and ruling, God is robed and surging with strength.

We cover ourselves with clothes, but God is clothed in strength. He is ready and waiting to give us the special covering of His love that we need.

november 1

Psalm 93: 2
"God the King" (GNB)

KJV: Thy throne is established of old; thou art from everlasting.

NISV: Your throne was established long ago; you are from all eternity.

GNB: Your throne, O Lord, has been firm from the beginning, and you existed before time began.

TMB: And yes, the world is firm, immovable, your throne ever firm—your eternal!

When was the beginning of God or the universe? Even the most brilliant scientists can't find a date for the beginning of time. As they study more about the universe, many are convinced that there is a God and He created all that is here. They will not find a beginning or an end. God has always been here and will always be here.

november 2

Psalm 93:3
"God the King" (GNB)

KJV: The floods have lifted up, O LORD, the floods have lifted up their voice; the floods lift up their waves.

NISV: The seas have lifted up, O LORD, the seas have lifted up their voice; the seas have lifted up their pounding waves.

GNB: The ocean depths. Raise their voice, O LORD; they raise their voice and roar.

TMB: Sea storms are up, God. Sea storms wild and roaring. Sea storms with thunderous breakers.

Are the floods and disasters of this earth stronger than our God? We cannot fight against the raging sea; God will take care of it. He will take care of all the oceans, storms, and disasters. God does not promise that we will never have problems; He promises us that He will be with us and see us through.

november 3

Psalm 93:4
"God the King" (GNB)

KJV: The LORD on high is mightier than the noise of many waters, yea, than the mighty waves of the sea.

NISV: Mightier than the thunder of the great waters, mightier than the breakers of the sea—the LORD on high is mighty.

GNB: The LORD rules supreme in heaven, greater than the roar of the ocean, more powerful than the waves of the sea.

TMB: Stronger than wild sea storms, Mightier than sea-storm breakers, Mighty God rules from High Heaven.

We are thankful we can rely on God's power to rule the earth.
   "A Mighty Fortress is Our God" *is a beautiful song written many years ago by Martin Luther. The words remind us of the power and might of God. The lyrics still ring true today:* "A mighty fortress is our God, A bulwark never failing; Our helper He, a-mid the flood of Mortal ills prevailing. …God's truth abideth still, His kingdom is forever."

november 4

Psalm 93:5
"God the King" (GNB)

KJV: The testimonies are very sure; holiness, becometh thine house, O Lord, for ever.

NISV: Your statutes stand firm; holiness adorns your house for endless days, O Lord.

GNB: Your laws are eternal, Lord, and your Temple is holy indeed, forever and ever.

TMB: What you say goes—it always has. "Beauty" and "Holy" mark your palace rule, God, to the very end of time.

When we follow Your word, You keep Your word to us. We know Your promises are the same, day after day. You don't change Your mind about us. We have witnessed Your holy power, and we know that when we call on You, You will answer our call.

This is a powerful psalm. Please enjoy reading the whole chapter of Psalm 93 from The Message Bible:

> God is King, robed and ruling, God is robed and surging with strength. And yes, the world is firm, immovable, your throne ever firm—you are eternal! Sea storms are up, God. Sea storms are wild and roaring. Sea storms with thunderous breakers. Stronger than wild sea storms, mightier than sea-storm breakers, Mighty God rules from High Heaven. What you say goes—it always has. "Beauty" and "Holy" mark your palace rule, God, to the very end of time.

november 5

Psalm 100:1
"A Hymn of Praise" (GNB)

Psalm 100 from The Message Bible is found on November 9.

KJV: Make a joyful noise unto the LORD, all ye lands.

NISV: Shout for joy to the LORD, all the earth.

GNB: Sing to the LORD, all the world!

TMB: On your feet now—applaud God!

Can you imagine how God could work in this world if all the nations would praise and worship him?
   How do you worship the Lord?

november 6

Psalm 100:2
"A Hymn of Praise" (GNB)

How should we worship the Lord?

KJV: Serve the LORD with gladness; come before his presence with singing.

NISV: Worship the LORD with gladness; come before him with joyful songs.

GNB: Worship the LORD with joy; come before him with happy songs!

TMB: Bring a gift of laughter, sing yourselves into his presence.

Whether we are in church, at home or driving down the street in the car, we can praise the Lord.

We will receive His strength. He will bless us through our songs and praise to Him.

november 7

Psalm 100:3
"A Hymn of Praise" (GNB)

KJV: Know ye that the LORD he is God: it is he that hath made us and not we ourselves; we are his people, and the sheep of his pasture.

NISV: Know that the LORD is God. It is he who made us, and we are his we are his people, the sheep of his pasture.

GNB: Never forget that the LORD is God. He made us, and we belong to him; we are his people, we are his flock.

TMB: Know this: God is God, and God, *God*. He made us; we didn't make him. We're his people, his well-tended sheep.

Lord, keep us humble, and acknowledge that you are our God.
Ignite your spirit by choosing to follow the Lord. He will give you hope and peace.

november 8

Psalm 100:4
"A Hymn of Praise" (GNB)

KJV: Enter into his gates with thanksgiving, and into his courts with praise; be thankful unto him, and bless his name.

NISV: Enter his gates with thanksgiving and his courts with praise; give thanks to him and praise his name.

GNB: Enter the Temple gates with praise. Give thanks to him and praise him.

TMB: Enter with the password: "Thank you!" Make yourselves at home, talking praise. Thank him. Worship him.

We can never give God enough praise and thanks. Our praise should be continuous for all the things He has given us.

november 9

Psalm 100:5
"A Hymn of Praise" (GNB)

KJV: For the LORD is good; his mercy is everlasting; and his truth endures to all generations.

NISV: For the LORD is good and his love endures forever; his faithfulness continues through all generations.

GNB: The LORD is good; his love is eternal and his faithfulness lasts forever.

TMB: For God is sheer beauty, all-generous in love, loyal always and ever.

Thank You, Lord, for each day You give us to live. Help us find the purpose of our lives.

Psalms 100 from The Message Bible:

On your feet now—applaud God! Bring a gift of laughter, sing yourselves into his presence. Know this: God is God, and God, *God*. He made us; we didn't make him. We're his people, his well-tended sheep. Enter with the password: "Thank you!" Make yourselves at home, talking praise. Thank him. Worship him. For God is sheer beauty, all-generous in love, loyal always and ever.

november 10

Proverbs 10:1
"Solomon's Proverbs" (GNB)

Chapter 10 of Proverbs is on December 10.

KJV: The proverbs of Solomon. A wise son maketh a glad father, but a foolish son is the heaviness of his mother.

NISV: A wise son brings joy to this father, but a foolish son grief to his mother.

GNB: These are Solomon's proverbs: A wise son makes his father proud of him; a foolish one brings his mother grief.

TMB: Wise son, glad father; stupid son, sad mother.

Help us make our earthly parents and heavenly Father proud of us.

november 11

Proverbs 10:2
"Solomon's Proverbs" (GNB)

KJV: Treasures of wickedness profit nothing: but righteousness delivereth from death.

NISV: Ill-gotten treasurers are of no value, but righteousness delivers from death.

GNB: Wealth you get by dishonesty will do you no good, but honesty can save your life.

TMB: Ill-gotten gain gets you nowhere; an honest life is immortal.

Lord, help us to think and pray. Stop us from doing things that will get us into trouble.

november 12

Proverbs 10:3
"Solomon's Proverbs" (GNB)

KJV: The LORD will not suffer the soul of the righteous to famish but he casteth away the substance of the wicked.

NISV: The LORD does not let the righteous go hungry but he thwarts the craving of the wicked.

GNB: The LORD will not let good people go hungry, but he will keep the wicked from getting what they want.

TMB: God won't starve an honest soul, but he frustrates the appetites of the wicked.

If we trust the Lord to fill our spiritual lives and take care of our bodily well being, we can be assured that He will save and protect us.

november 13

Proverbs 10:4
"Solomon's Proverbs" (GNB)

KJV: He becometh poor that dealeth with a slack hand: but the hand of the diligent maketh rich.

NISV: Lazy hands make a man poor, but diligent hands bring wealth.

GNB: Being lazy will make you poor, but hard work will make you rich.

TMB: Sloth makes you poor; diligence brings wealth.

As we go through each day make our work worthy of Your praise.

november 14

Proverbs 10:5
"Solomon's Proverbs" (GNB)

KJV: He that gathereth in summer is a wise son: but he that sleepeth in harvest is a son that causeth shame.

NISV: He who gathers crops in summer is a wise son, but he who sleeps during harvest is a disgraceful son.

GNB: A sensible man gathers the crops when they are ready; it is a disgrace to sleep through the time of harvest.

TMB: Make hay while the sun shines—that's smart; go fishing during harvest—that's stupid.

The harvest of souls is great. Lord, help us to see the need of the people around us. Show us how and when to reach them.

Ignite your spirit with the things of the Lord, and He will show you who needs your care.

november 15

Proverbs 10:6
"Solomon's Proverbs" (GNB)

KJV: Blessings are upon the head of the just: but violence covereth the mouth of the wicked.

NISV: Blessings crown the head of the righteous, but violence overwhelms the mouth of the wicked.

GNB: A good man will receive blessings. A wicked man's words hide a violent nature.

TMB: Blessings accrue on a good and honest life, but the mouth of the wicked is a dark cave of abuse.

These are the blessings that the Lord promises us from the song "Showers of Blessing"

There shall be showers of blessing. This is the promise of love; There shall be seasons refreshing Sent from the Saviour above,…Precious, reviving again, Over the hills and the valley, Sound of abundance of rain.…Grant to us now a refreshing; Come, and now honor Thy Word. Showers,…of blessing, Showers of blessing we need; Mercy drops round us are falling, But for the showers we plead.

"There Shall Be Showers of Blessing" words by Daniel W. Whittle, music by James McGranahan.

Please bless us according to Your grace, love, and mercy.

november 16

Proverbs 10:7
"Solomon's Proverbs" (GNB)

KJV: The memory of the just is blessed: but the name of the wicked shall rot.

NISV: The memory of the righteous will be a blessing, but the name of the wicked will rot.

GNB: Good people will be remembered as a blessing, but the wicked will soon be forgotten.

TMB: A good and honest life is a blessed memorial; a wicked life leaves a rotten stench.

When you think of friends that have passed away, what do you remember?

How do you want to be remembered when you are no longer on this earth? Your actions now will be your legacy. Will your life be remembered as a blessing to those around you?

Write what you think your legacy might be.

november 17

Proverbs 10:8
"Solomon's Proverbs" (GNB)

KJV: The wise in heart will receive commandments: but a prating fool shall fall.

NISV: The wise in heart accept commands, but a chattering fool comes to ruin.

GNB: Sensible people accept good advice. People who talk foolishly will come to ruin.

TMB: A wise heart takes orders; an empty head will come unglued.

Do we listen to what God commands us to do? If we take God's advice He will bless us.

november 18

Proverbs 10:9
"Solomon's Proverbs" (GNB)

KJV: He that walketh uprightly walketh surely: but he that perverteth his ways shall be known.

NISV: The man of integrity walks securely, but he who takes crooked paths will be found out.

GNB: Honest people are safe and secure, but the dishonest will be caught.

TMB: Honesty lives confident and carefree, but Shifty is sure to be exposed.

We see the evidence of those who are out to destroy themselves and others. They will be caught. Maybe not caught by human measures, but God will deal with them.

november 19

Proverbs 10:10
"Solomon's Proverbs" (GNB)

KJV: He that winketh with the eye causeth sorrow: but a prating fool shall fall.

NISV: He who winks maliciously causes grief, and a chattering fool comes to ruin.

GNB: Someone who holds back the truth causes trouble, but one who openly criticizes works for peace.

TMB: An evasive eye is a sign of trouble ahead, but an open, face-to-face meeting results in peace.

How do you handle those awkward situations when you know the truth but are afraid to tell the truth? God will help us set the record straight if we ask for His help.

november 20

Proverbs 10:11
"Solomon's Proverbs" (GNB)

KJV: The mouth of a righteous man is a well of life: but violence covereth the mouth of the wicked.

NISV: The mouth of the righteous is a fountain of life, but violence overwhelms the mouth of the wicked.

GNB: A good man's words are a fountain of life, but a wicked man's words hide a violent nature.

TMB: The mouth of a good person is a deep, life-giving well, but the mouth of the wicked is a dark cave of abuse.

Be careful what you say. No matter who you are talking to, there is no dead end to gossip and rumor. Don't say anything you don't want repeated and you won't regret it later. You may hear your story later and it probably won't sound anything like you what thought you said.

Be careful what you write in any form, especially emails or on websites. Once something is in writing it can't be taken back.

Can you think of something you wish you didn't say or write?

november 21

Proverbs 10:12
"Solomon's Proverbs" (gnb)

KJV: Hatred stirreth up strifes: but love covereth all sins.

NISV: Hatred stirs up dissension, but love covers over all wrongs.

GNB: Hate stirs up trouble, but love forgives all offenses.

TMB: Hatred starts fights, but love pulls a quilt over the bickering.

Loving all people all the time is very hard to do. But if hatred takes over you will pay the penalty in your own life. Instead of letting the strife and bad feelings you have toward someone hurt you, turn the energy into something useful to help the person. They won't know how to react and you will feel much better for doing good and not plotting against them. Positive action leads to positive feedback.

If you are having a hard time loving a certain person, write their name down, and pray for them. You will be surprised how it will change your attitude.

Lord, help us to find positive things about those around us. Help us to learn to love those who are hard to love.

As suggested on an earlier date, make a prayer box by putting a slit in the top of a box. Put your prayer requests on a slip of paper and put them in the box. Check it weekly or monthly and see how your prayers are being answered.

november 22

Proverbs 10:13
"Solomon's Proverbs" (GNB)

KJV: In the lips of him that hath understanding wisdom is found but a rod is for the back of him that is void of understanding.

NISV: Wisdom is found on the lips of the discerning, but a rod is for the back of him who lacks judgment.

GNB: Intelligent people talk sense, but stupid people need to be punished.

TMB: You'll find wisdom on the lips of a person of insight, but the shortsighted needs a slap in the face.

Before you speak, be sure you know the details.

november 23

Proverbs 10:14
"Solomon's Proverbs" (GNB)

KJV: Wise men lay up knowledge: but the mouth of the foolish is near destruction.

NISV: Wise men store up knowledge, but the mouth of a fool invites ruin.

GNB: The wise get all the knowledge they can, but when fools speak, trouble is not far off.

TMB: The wise accumulate knowledge—a true treasure; know-it-alls talk too much—a sheer waste.

Study the subject and know the facts. Do not let anyone make you look foolish.

november 24

Proverbs 10:15
"Solomon's Proverbs" (GNB)

KJV: The rich man's wealth is his strong city: The destruction of the poor is their poverty.

NISV: The wealth of the rich is their fortified city, but poverty is the ruin of the poor.

GNB: Wealth protects the rich; poverty destroys the poor.

TMB: The Road to Life Is a Disciplined Life." The wealth of the rich is their bastion; the poverty of the indigent is their ruin.

To be spiritually rich is to guarantee your future. No matter how much money you have, there is no guarantee it will be there in the future. Trust God with your future; His way is the only way to be secure.

november 25

Proverbs 10:16
"Solomon's Proverbs" (GNB)

KJV: The labour of the righteous tendeth to life: the fruit of the wicked to sin.

NISV: The wages of the righteous bring them life, but the income of the wicked brings them punishment.

GNB: The reward for doing good is life, but sin leads only to more sin.

TMB: The wage of a good person is exuberant life; an evil person ends up with nothing but sin.

When you do something nice for someone, it not only helps them, but your reward is in knowing that you have accomplished doing good and helping that person. When we gossip or do bad things to people, it can only end up doing harm. Pray and ask God to help you to help others and to keep you from getting into bad situations.

november 26

Proverbs 10:17–18
"Solomon's Proverbs" (GNB)

KJV: He is in the way of life that keepeth instruction: but he that refuseth reproof erreth. ¹⁸ He that hideth hatred with lying lips, and he that uttereth a slander, is a fool.

NISV: He who heeds discipline shows the way to life, but whoever ignores correction leads others astray. ¹⁸ He who conceals his hatred has lying lips, and whoever spreads slander is a fool.

GNB: People who listen when they are corrected will live, but those who will not admit that they are wrong are in danger. ¹⁸ A man who hides his hatred is a liar. Anyone who spreads gossip is a fool.

TMB: The road to life is a disciplined life; ignore correction and you're lost for good. Liars secretly hoard hatred; fools openly spread slander.

Do you remember when someone tried to get you to listen to them and do the "right" thing? What happened when you did the opposite? It is better to listen and not be stubborn. The consequences of "doing it your way" may last forever. When you hold a grudge and hate someone, it hurts you more than it hurts that person. They may not know your feelings, so it will not affect them. Holding all this hate and anger inside will create bitterness and eat you up. Let go and let God take away the bad feelings—what good can come from hanging onto them?

Is there someone you need to forgive so you can get on with life?

november 27

Proverbs 10:19
"Solomon's Proverbs" (GNB)

KJV: In the multitude of words there wanteth not sin: but he that refraineth his lips is wise.

NISV: When words are many, sin is not absent, but he who holds his tongue is wise.

GNB: The more you talk, the more likely you are to sin. If you are wise, you will keep quiet.

TMB: The more talk, the less truth; the wise measure their words.

Do you talk to hear yourself talk? Listen to others and hear what they are saying. You will learn more about the other person and understand them better. Some of the things we feel are best left unsaid.

Can you think of someone you think listens to you? Would you like to be more like that person? Ask God to help you become a better listener.

november 28

Proverbs 10:20
"Solomon's Proverbs" (GNB)

KJV: The tongue of the just is as choice silver: the heart of the wicked is little worth.

NISV: The tongue of the righteous is choice silver, but the heart of the wicked is of little value.

GNB: A good man's words are like pure silver; a wicked man's ideas are worthless.

TMB: The speech of a good person is worth waiting for; the blabber of the wicked is worthless.

When you speak, do others listen? If they don't, maybe you should think more about what you say before you say it.

In conflict resolution individuals are taught to repeat back to others what they thought the person was trying to say. What we mean to say and what someone hears may not be the same thing. So try repeating back to people what you think you heard so you both understand what is being said.

God will help you speak the truth; ask Him for guidance.

november 29

Proverbs 10:21
"Solomon's Proverbs" (GNB)

KJV: The lips of the righteous feed many: but fools die for want of wisdom.

NISV: The lips of the righteous nourish many, but fools die for lack of judgment.

GNB: A good man's words will benefit many people, but you can kill yourself with stupidity.

TMB: The talk of a good person is rich fare for many, but chatterboxes die of an empty heart.

Does the Lord Jesus control what you say? Pray and ask Him for His help.

november 30

Proverbs 10:22
"Solomon's Proverbs" (GNB)

KJV: The blessing of the LORD, it maketh rich, and he addeth no sorrow with it.

NISV: The blessing of the LORD brings wealth, and he adds not trouble to it.

GNB: It is the LORD's blessing that makes you wealthy. Hard work can make you no richer.

TMB: "Fear-of-God Expands Your Life." God's blessing makes life rich; nothing we do can improve on God.

Ask God for His blessings each day. God is waiting for us to ask. Consider everything you do God's business, and He will help you every moment of every day.

december 1

Proverbs 10:23
"Solomon's Proverbs" (GNB)

KJV: It is as sport to a fool to do mischief: but a man of understanding hath wisdom.

NISV: A fool finds pleasure in evil conduct, but a man of understanding delights in wisdom.

GNB: It is foolish to enjoy doing wrong. Intelligent people take pleasure in wisdom.

TMB: An empty-head thinks mischief is fun, but a mindful person relishes wisdom.

Have you ever watched someone do something evil or just plain mean? Pray for that person because he needs God's help!

december 2

Proverbs 10:24
"Solomon's Proverbs" (GNB)

KJV: The fear of the wicked, it shall come upon him: but the desire of the righteous shall be granted.

NISV: What the wicked dreads will overtake him; what the righteous desire will be granted.

GNB: The righteous get what they want, but the wicked will get what they fear most.

TMB: The nightmares of the wicked come true; what the good people desire, they get.

When we pray for others, we may not see the results. God will take care of every situation. Trust Him to make everything work out right.

december 3

Proverbs 10:25
"Solomon's Proverbs" (gnb)

KJV: As the whirlwind passeth, so is the wicked no more: but the righteous is an everlasting foundation.

NISV: When the storm has swept by, the wicked are gone, but the righteous stand firm forever.

GNB: Storms come, and the wicked are blown away, but honest people are always safe.

TMB: When the storm is over, there's nothing left of the wicked; good people, firm on their rock foundation, aren't even fazed.

Do you have a personal relationship with Jesus? Think of those who don't have anything to believe in. How lost and alone they must feel. They do things because the only driving force in their lives is selfishness and self-gratification, which comes from evil forces of this world.

God, help us to pray for those who don't know You. We hope they can find the peace and comfort You give to us.

Has your soul been ignited with the fire of God? If you want this assurance today, pray and ask Jesus to be the center of your life. Confess your sins, and He will forgive your sins. Believe and receive all He offers you.

Look at website www.Jesus2020.com.

december 4

Proverbs 10:26
"Solomon's Proverbs" (GNB)

KJV: As vinegar to the teeth, and as smoke to the eyes, so is the sluggard to them that send him.

NISV: As vinegar to the teeth and smoke to the eyes, so is a sluggard to those who send him.

GNB: Never get a lazy man to do something for you' he will be as irritating as vinegar on your teeth or smoke in your eyes.

TMB: A lazy employee will give you nothing but trouble; it's vinegar in the mouth, smoke in the eyes.

When there is a job to be done, it is better to do it yourself to make sure it is done right.

december 5

Proverbs 10:27
"Solomon's Proverbs" (GNB)

KJV: The fear of the Lord prolongeth days: but the years of the wicked shall be shortened.

NISV: The fear of the Lord adds length to life, but the years of the wicked are cut short.

GNB: Have reverence for the Lord, and you will live longer. The wicked die before their time.

TMB: The Fear-of-God expands your life; a wicked life is a puny life.

A recent poll about the longevity of life and church attendance was published. It showed that "church attendees" have longer life spans than others. The connection with God and those who worship God gives peace and harmony to life that nothing else can do. Not just the "fear of the Lord" but the worship of the Lord adds to the richness of life that only God can give.

december 6

Proverbs 10:28
"Solomon's Proverbs" (GNB)

KJV: The hope of the righteous shall be gladness: but the expectation of the wicked shall perish.

NISV: The prospect of the righteous is joy, but the hopes of the wicked come to nothing.

GNB: The hopes of good men lead to joy, but wicked people can look forward to nothing.

TMB: The aspirations of good people end in celebration; the ambitions of bad people crash.

Because we have the promise of eternal life, we can live each day to the fullest. God will take care of us at the end of our earthly life. If you don't have that hope, just ask Jesus to come into your heart and to forgive you of your sins and He will do it. You don't have to do anything but believe in Him and trust Him. He already took care of our sins on the cross. Read John 3:16.

december 7

Proverbs 10:29
"Solomon's Proverbs" (GNB)

KJV: The way of the LORD is strength to the upright: but destruction shall be to the workers of iniquity.

NISV: The way of the LORD is a refuge for the righteous, but it is the ruin of those who do evil.

GNB: The LORD protects honest people, but destroys those who do wrong.

TMB: God is solid backing to a well-lived life, but he calls into question a shabby performance.

If we do what God asks and believe in Him, He will give us everything we need to survive every day.

december 8

Proverbs 10:30
"Solomon's Proverbs" (GNB)

KJV: The righteous shall never be removed: but the wicked shall not inhabit the earth.

NISV: The righteous will never be uprooted, but the wicked will not remain in the land.

GNB: Righteous people will always have security, but the wicked will not survive in the land.

TMB: Good people last—they can't be moved; the wicked are here today, gone tomorrow.

When God is your guide and you let Him take control of your life, you can depend on His promises. This doesn't mean everything will be perfect, but He will be there to give you strength.

december 9

Proverbs 10:31
"Solomon's Proverbs" (GNB)

KJV: The mouth of the just bringeth forth wisdom: but the froward tongue shall be cut out.

NISV: The mouth of the righteous brings forth wisdom, but a perverse tongue will be cut out.

GNB: Righteous people speak wisdom, but the tongue that speaks evil will be stopped.

TMB: A good person's mouth is a clear fountain; a foul mouth is a stagnant swamp.

Only God can put the right words in your mouth. Only He can help you speak with wisdom. Trust God to help you say the right thing before you speak.

Can you think of a time that God gave you the right words to say?

december 10

Proverbs 10:32
"Solomon's Proverbs"

KJV: The lips of the righteous know what is acceptable: but the mouth of the wicked speaketh frowardness.

NISV: The lips of the righteous know what is fitting, but the mouth of the wicked only what is perverse.

GNB: Righteous people know the kind thing to say, but the wicked are always saying things that hurt.

TMB: The speech of a good person clears the air, the words of the wicked pollute it.

The damage we do when if we speak unkind words to people will stay with the person long after we leave. The good words that we say will brighten their day. Love that we show with our words will endure us to our friends forever.

Which way do you wish to be remembered?

I hope you enjoy reading this chapter of Proverbs 10 from NISV:

A wise son brings joy to this father, but a foolish son grief to his mother. Ill-gotten treasures are of no value, but righteousness delivers from death. The Lord does not let the righteous go hungry but he thwarts the craving of the wicked. Lazy hands make a man poor, but diligent hands bring wealth. He who gathers crops in summer is a wise son, but who he sleeps during harvest is a disgraceful son. Blessings crown the head of the righteous, but violence overwhelms the mouth of the wicked. The memory of the righteous will be a blessing, but the name of the wicked will rot. The wise in heart accept commands, but a chattering fool comes to ruin. The man of integrity walks securely, but he who takes crooked paths will be found out. He who winks maliciously causes grief, and a chattering fool comes to ruin. The mouth of the righteous is a fountain of life, but violence overwhelms the mouth of the wicked. Hatred stirs up dissension, but love covers over all wrongs. Wisdom is found on the lips of the discerning, but a rod is for the back of him who lacks judgment. Wise men store up knowledge, but the mouth of a fool invites ruin. The wages of the righteous bring them life, but the income of the wicked brings them punishment. He who heeds discipline shows the way to life, but whoever ignores correction leads others astray. He who conceals his hatred has lying lips, and whoever spreads slander is a fool. When words are many, sin is not absent, but he who holds his tongue is wise. The tongue of the righteous is choice silver, but the heart of the wicked is of little value. The lips of the righteous nourish many, but fools die for lack of judgment. The blessing of the Lord brings wealth, and he adds not trouble to it. A fool finds pleasure in evil conduct, but a man of understanding delights in wisdom. What the wicked dreads will overtake him; what the righteous desire will be granted. When the storm has swept by, the wicked are gone, but the righteous stand firm forever. As vinegar to the teeth and smoke to the eyes, so is a sluggard to those who send him. The fear of the Lord adds length to life, but the years of the wicked are cut short. The prospect of the righteous is joy, but the hopes of the wicked come to nothing. The way of the Lord is a refuge for the righteous, but it is the ruin of those who do evil. The righteous will never be uprooted, but the wicked will not remain in the land. The mouth of the righteous brings forth wisdom, but a perverse tongue will be cut out. The lips of the righteous know what is fitting, but the mouth of the wicked only what is perverse.

december 11

Hebrews 1:1
"God's word through His Son" (GNB)

December 11 to 24 is from Hebrews 1 (TMB)
See December 24th for the whole chapter.

- KJV: God who at sundry times and in divers manners spake in time past unto the Fathers by the prophets;

- NISV: In the past God spoke to our forefathers through the prophets at many times and in various ways.

- GNB: In the past God spoke to our ancestors many times and in many ways through the prophets.

- TMB: Going through a long line of prophets, God has been addressing our ancestors in different ways for centuries.

Who are the prophets today? Can we trust them? Only those who believe in Jesus Christ dying on the cross to forgive our sins and who believe in the cleansing blood of Jesus are true prophets. Any other teaching is not of God. Only the supreme God of Abraham can perform miracles that we need.

december 12

Hebrews 1:2
"God's word through His Son" (GNB)

KJV: *[God]…hath in these last days spoken unto us by his Son, whom he hath appointed heir of all things, by whom also he made the worlds:*

NISV: *…but in these last days he [God] has spoken to us by his Son, whom he appointed heir of all things, and through whom he made the universe.*

GNB: *…but in these last days he [God] has spoken to us through his Son. He is the one through whom God created the universe, the one whom God has chosen to possess all things at the end.*

TMB: *Recently he [God] spoke to us directly through his Son. By his son, God created the world in the beginning, and it will all belong to the Son at the end.*

We know why Jesus came to earth and how He has saved us from our sins. All we need to do is ask Jesus to come into our hearts and lives and He will do it. We do not earn salvation by good deeds or any other way. "He is the way, the truth and the life" (John 14:6).

december 13

Hebrews 1:3
"God's word through His Son" (GNB)

KJV: Who being the brightness of his glory, and the express image of his person, and upholding all things by the word of his power, when he had by himself purged our sins, sat down on the right hand of the Majesty on high.

NISV: The Son is the radiance of God's glory and the exact representation of his being, sustaining all things by his powerful word. After he had provided purification for sins, he sat down at the right hand of the Majesty in heaven.

GNB: He reflects the brightness of God's glory and is the exact likeness of God's own being, sustaining the universe with his powerful word. After achieving forgiveness for the sins of mankind, he sat down in heaven at the right side of God, the Supreme Power.

TMB: This Son perfectly mirrors God, and is stamped with God's nature. He holds everything together by what he says—powerful words!

Dear Lord, we thank You for sending Jesus to save us from our sins. Thank You for the grace and power You provide us daily to live in this world. Help us to be worthy of all the things You have given us.

december 14

Hebrews 1:4
"God's word through His Son" (GNB)

KJV: Being made so much better than the angels, as he hath by inheritance obtained a more excellent name than they.

NISV: So he became as much superior to the angels as the name he has inherited is superior to theirs.

GNB: The Son was made greater than the angels, just as the name that God gave him is greater than theirs.

TMB: "The Son is Higher than Angels." After he finished the sacrifice for sins, the Son took his honored place high in the heaven, right alongside God, far higher that any angel in rank and rule.

Thank You again for giving us Your Son, Jesus. Teach us how to worship and honor You according to Your words in the Bible. Thank You for forgiving us when we fail You.

december 15

Hebrews 1:5
"God's word through His Son" (gnb)

KJV: For unto which of the angels said he at any time, Thou art my son, this day have I begotten thee? And again, I will be to him a Father, and he shall be to me a Son?

NISV: For to which of the angels did God ever say, "You are my Son; today I have become your Father? Or again, "I will be his Father, and he will be my Son"?

GNB: For God never said to any of his angels, "You are my Son; today I have become your Father." Nor did God say about any angel, I will be his Father, and he will be my Son."

TMB: Did God ever, say to an angel, "You're my Son; today I celebrate you"? Or, "I'm his Father, he's my Son"?

God put His Son, Jesus, higher than any angel. We are not to worship angels but the Trinity—God, Son, and Holy Spirit. God will send His angel to protect us, but we are not to worship them. It really is God who is doing the protecting—His angels are His servants to us.

I think the Holy Spirit is sometimes what we perceive as being angels.

december 16

Hebrews 1:6
"God's word through His Son"

KJV: And again, when he bringeth in the first begotten unto the world, he saith, And let all the angels of God worship him.

NISV: And again, when God brings his firstborn into the world, he says, "Let all God's angels worship him."

GNB: But when God was about to send his first-born Son into the world, he said, "All of God's angels must worship him."

TMB: When he presents his honored Son to the world, he says, "All angels must worship him."

All the angels in God's heaven cannot do anything unless God gives the order. Thank You, God, for sending Your angels to help us.

The song "Holy, Holy, Holy!" *comes to mind when reading this chapter of Hebrews. The words are* "Holy, Holy, Holy! Lord God Almighty! Early in the morning our song will rise to Thee…Holy, Holy, Holy! Merciful and mighty! God in Three Persons blessed Trinity…Cheribim and seraphim falling down before Thee, Which wert and art, and evermore shalt be…Only thou art Holy; there is none beside Thee Perfect in power and love, and purity.…God in Three Persons blessed Trinity." "Holy, Holy, Holy!" *words by Reginald Heber and music by John B Dykes.*

december 17

Hebrews 1:7
"God's word through His Son" (GNB)

KJV: And of the angels he saith, who maketh his angels spirits, and his ministers a flame of fire.

NISV: In speaking of the angels he says, "He makes his angels winds, his servants flames of fire."

GNB: But about the angels God said, "God makes his angels winds, and his servants flames of fire."

TMB: Regarding angels he says, The messengers are winds, the servants are tongues of fire.

Do you feel God's presence close to you? Pray and ask Him to help you through each day. He will send His angels to your rescue.

december 18

Hebrews 1:8
"God's word through His Son" (GNB)

KJV: But unto the Son he saith, Thy throne, O God, is for ever and ever: a scepter of righteousness is the scepter of thy kingdom.

NISV: But about the Son he says, "Your throne, O God, will last for ever and ever, and righteousness will be the scepter of your kingdom."

GNB: About the Son, however, God said: "Your kingdom, O God, will last forever and ever!"

TMB: But he says to the Son, You're God, and on the throne for good; your rule makes everything right.

God and His Son, have the world in their "hands." We don't know what the future holds, but they have complete control of the future. Put your trust in God. He will ignite the fire of God in you and give you great blessings.

december 19

Hebrews 1:9
"God's word through His Son" (GNB)

KJV: Thou hast loved righteousness, and hated iniquity; therefore God, even thy God, hath anointed thee with the oil of gladness above thy fellows.

NISV: You have loved righteousness and hated wickedness; therefore God, your God, has set you above your companions by anointing you with the oil of joy.

GNB: You love what is right and hate what is wrong. That is why God, your God, has chosen you and has given you the honor far greater than he gave to your companions."

TMB: You love it when things are right; you hate it when things are wrong. That is why God, your God, poured fragrant oil on your head, Marking you out as king, far above your dear companions.

God gave authority to His Son to become the King of kings and Lord of lords.

What other gods do you worship? Does this worship give you peace? Only Jesus, through God and the Holy Spirit can give you real peace.

december 20

Hebrews 1:10
"God's word through His Son" (GNB)

KJV: And, Thou, LORD, in the beginning hast laid the foundation of the earth; and the heavens are the works of thine hands.

NISV: He also says, "In the beginning, O LORD, you laid the foundations of the earth, and the heavens are the work of your hands."

GNB: He also said, "You, LORD, in the beginning created the earth, and with your own hands you made the heavens."

TMB: And again to the Son, You, Master, started it all, laid earth's foundations, then created the stars in the sky. Earth and sky will wear out, but not you;

A favorite hymn of all time is "How Great Thou Art" written by Carl Boberg, and Translated by S. K. Hine. Copyright 1954 by Dr. N. A. Woychuk to Alfred B. Smith. This was a Swedish Melody, Revised by Jean Staneschi, 1929.

"O, Lord my God! When I in awesome wonder Consider all the works Thy hands have made, I see the stars, I hear the mighty thunder, Thy pow'r thro' out the universe displayed.[...verse 2–3] When Christ shall come with-shout of acclamation And take me home-what joy shall fill my heart! Then I shall bow in humble adoration, And there proclaim, my God, how great Thou art!

"Then sings my soul my Savior God to Thee, How great Thou art, how great Thou art! Then sings my soul, my Savior God to Thee, How great Thou art, how great Thou art!" This beautiful hymn was written in Sweden in 1886. Later in Romania, Jean Staneschi simplified the melody and published it in the Romanian Baptist Hymnal in 1929. This English translation was published in America in 1954 by Dr. N. A. Woychuk in his book "Making Melody".

Thank You, Lord, for the beautiful world You have given us. Help us to treat the earth with respect.

december 21

Hebrews 1:11
"God's word through His Son" (GNB)

KJV: *[The earth and things of the earth.]* They shall perish; but thou remainest; and they all shall wax old as doth a garment;

NISV: *[The earth and things of the earth.]* They will perish, but you remain; they will all wear out like a garment.

GNB: *[The earth and things of the earth.]* They will disappear, but you will remain; they will all wear out like clothes.

TMB: *[The earth and things of the earth.]*...they become threadbare like an old coat;

We trust all You do. We know that You were here from the beginning and will be here long after this physical world is gone. Thank You for all things.

december 22

Hebrews 1:12
"God's word through His Son" (GNB)

KJV: *[Things of the earth.]*…And as a vesture shalt thou fold them up, and they shall be changed; but thou art the same and thy years shall not fail.

NISV: *[Things of the earth.]*…"You will roll them up like robe; like a garment they will be changed. But you remain the same, and your years will never end."

GNB: *[Things of the earth.]*…"You will fold them up like a coat, and they will be changed like clothes. But you are always the same, and your life never ends."

TMB: *[Things of the earth.]*…You'll fold them up like a worn-out cloak, and lay them away on the shelf. But you'll stay the same, year after year; you'll never fade, you'll never wear out.

Even though the physical world as we know it will change; we know that God does not change. His promises are forever.

december 23

Hebrews 1:13
"God's word through His Son" (GNB)

KJV: But to which of the angels said he at any time. Sit on my right hand, until I make thine enemies thy footstool?

NISV: To which of the angels did God ever say, "Sit at my right hand until I make your enemies a footstool for your feet."

GNB: God never said to any of his angels: "Sit here at my right side until I put your enemies as a footstool under your feet."

TMB: And did he ever say anything like this to an angel? Sit alongside me here on my throne until I make your enemies a stool for your feet.

Only the trinity—God the Father, Jesus the Son, and the Holy Spirit—is in charge of the world. The angels worship God and are at His service. Thank You, God, for being our only God. We know You rule the world.

december 24

Hebrews 1:14
"God's word through His Son" (GNB)

KJV: Are they not all ministering spirits, sent forth to minister for them who shall be heirs of salvation?

NISV: Are not all angels ministering spirits sent to serve those who will inherit salvation?

GNB: What are the angels, then? They are spirits who serve God and are sent by him to help those who are to receive salvation.

TMB: Isn't it obvious that all angels are sent to help out with those lined up to receive salvation?

The complete chapter on December 11 to 24, Hebrews 1 from The Message Bible:

Going through a long line of prophets, God has been addressing our ancestors in different ways for centuries. Recently he spoke to us directly through his Son. By his son, God created the world in the beginning, and it will all belong to the Son at the end. This Son perfectly mirrors God, and is stamped with God's nature. He holds everything together by what he says—powerful words!

The Son is Higher than Angels. After he finished the sacrifice for sins, the Son took his honored place high in the heaven, right alongside God, far higher that any angel in rank and rule. Did

God ever, say to an angel, "You're my Son; today I celebrate you"? Or, "I'm his Father, he's my Son"? When he presents his honored Son to the world, he says, "All angels must worship him."

Regarding angels he says, The messengers are winds, the servants are tongues of fire.

But he says to the Son, you're God, and on the throne for good, your rule makes everything right. You love it when things are right; you hate it when things are wrong. That is why God, your God, poured fragrant oil on your head, Marking you out as king, far above your dear companions. And again to the Son, You, Master, started it all, laid earth's foundations, then created the stars in the sky. Earth and sky will wear out, but not you; they become threadbare like an old coat; You'll fold them up like a worn-out cloak, and lay them away on the shelf. But you'll stay the same, year after year; you'll never fade, you'll never wear out. And did he ever say anything like this to an angel? Sit alongside me here on my throne until I make your enemies a stool for your feet. Isn't it obvious that all angels are sent to help out with those lined up to receive salvation?

Thank You for sending Your angels to us to help us in our daily struggles.

december 25

Luke 2:6–7
The story of God sending His Son, our Savior, to earth.

Luke 2 from the Message Bible is on December 31ˢᵗ.

KJV: ⁶ And so it was, that, while they were there, [in Bethlehem] the days were accomplished that she should be delivered. ⁷ And she brought forth her firstborn son, and wrapped him in swaddling clothes, and laid him in a manger because there was no room for them in the inn.

NISV: ⁶ While they were there, the time came for the baby to be born, ⁷ and she gave birth to her firstborn, a son. She wrapped him in cloths and placed him in a manger, because there was no room for them in the inn.

GNB: ⁶...and while they were in Bethlehem, the time came for her to have her baby. ⁷ She gave birth to her first son, wrapped him in cloths and laid him in a manger—there was no room for them to stay in the inn.

TMB: ⁶ While they were there, the time came for her to give birth. She gave birth to a son, her firstborn. ⁷ She wrapped him in a blanket and laid him in a manger, because there was no room in the hostel.

Also Luke 2: 11 For unto you is born this day in the city of David a Saviour, which is Christ the Lord. (KJV)

Can you imagine how Mary and Joseph felt? This child was so special. He was the Son of God, yet there was no comfortable place for any baby to be born. I think God wanted us to know that Jesus came to save everyone, the rich and the poor—we are all special in His sight.

december 26

Luke 2:8
The story of God sending His Son, our Savior, to earth.

KJV: And there were in the same country shepherds abiding in the field, keeping watch over their flock by night.

NISV: And there were shepherds living out in the fields nearby, keeping watch over their flocks at night.

GNB: There were some shepherds in that part of the country who were spending the night in the fields, taking care of their flocks.

TMB: There were sheepherders camping in the neighborhood. They had set night watches over their sheep.

What a wonderful experience to be present when God announced Jesus' birth. What a day to be a shepherd! Can you imagine how the shepherds felt?

december 27

Luke 2:9–10
The story of God sending His Son, our Savior, to earth.

KJV: ⁹ And lo, the angel of the Lord came upon them (the shepherds) and the glory of the Lord shone round about them: and they were sore afraid. ¹⁰ And the angel said unto them, Fear not: for, behold, I bring you good tidings of great joy, which shall be to all people.

NISV: ⁹ An angel of the Lord appeared to them, and the glory of the Lord shone around them, and they were terrified. ¹⁰ But the angel said to them, "Do not be afraid. I bring you good news of great joy that will be for all the people."

GNB: ⁹ An angel of the Lord appeared to them, and the glory of the Lord shone over them. They were terribly afraid. ¹⁰ but the angel said to them, "Don't be afraid! I am here with good news for you, which will bring great joy to all the people."

TMB: Suddenly, God's angel stood among them and God's glory blazed around them. They were terrified. The angel said, "Don't be afraid. I'm here to announce a great and joyful event that is meant for everybody, worldwide…"

The shepherds were the only people that were given the announcement of Jesus' birth. What a sight it would have been to see the angels filling the heavens, singing and talking to the shepherds. How frightened and blessed these lowly shepherds must have been.

What would you have done if you were a shepherd that day?

december 28

Luke 2:11
The story of God sending His Son, our Savior, to earth.

KJV: For unto you is born this day in the city of David a Saviour, which is Christ the Lord.

NISV: Today in the town of David a Savior has been born to you; he is Christ the Lord.

GNB: This very day in David's town your Savior was born—Christ the Lord!

TMB: A Savior has just been born in David's town, a Savior who is Messiah and Master.

Few people knew at the time this baby was born that His was the most significant birth ever on our earth. Throughout the ages no birth has ever been celebrated more than that of Jesus Christ. He is the Savior of this world.

Is he the Savior of your life? He gives hope, love, joy, and peace that will never go away.

december 29

Luke 2:12
The story of God sending His Son, our Savior, to earth.

KJV: And this shall be a sign unto you; Ye shall find the babe wrapped in swaddling clothes, lying in a manger.

NISV: "This will be a sign to you: You will find a baby wrapped in cloths and lying in a manger."

GNB: "And this is what will prove it to you: you will find a baby wrapped in cloths and lying in a manger."

TMB: "This is what you're to look for: a baby wrapped in a blanket and lying in a manger."

When the shepherds and the wise men saw Jesus lying in the manger, they fell down and worshipped Him. How wonderful that we have the opportunity to worship and follow Jesus and to know that He is our Savior.

december 30

Luke 2:13
The story of God sending His Son, our Savior, to earth.

KJV: And suddenly there was with the angel a multitude of the heavenly host praising God, and saying...

NISV: Suddenly a great company of the heavenly host appeared with the angel, praising God and saying...

GNB: Suddenly a great army of heaven's angels appeared with the angel, singing praises to God...

TMB: At once the angel was joined by a huge angelic choir singing God' praises...

The overwhelming power and pride of God was shown that great day when Jesus was sent to earth. Help us to sing with the angels and worship Him.
  Browse www.Jesus2020.com to learn more about Him.

december 31

Luke 2:14
The story of God sending His Son, our Savior, to earth.

KJV: "Glory to God in the highest, and on earth peace, good will toward men."

NISV: "Glory to God in the highest, and on earth peace to men on whom his favor rests."

GNB: "Glory to God in the highest heaven, and peace on earth to those with whom he is pleased!"

TMB: Glory to God in the heavenly heights, Peace to all men and women on earth who please him.

Please enjoy reading the story of the birth of Jesus from December 25 to 31, Luke 2 from The Message Bible:

While they were there, the time came for her to give birth. She gave birth to a son, her firstborn. She wrapped him in a blanket and laid him in a manger, because there was no room in the hostel. There were sheepherders camping in the neighborhood. They had set night watches over their sheep. Suddenly, God's angel stood among them and God's glory blazed around them. They were terrified. The angel said, "Don't be afraid. I'm here to announce a great and joyful event that is meant for everybody, worldwide: A Savior has just been born in David's town, a Savior who is Messiah and Master. This is what you're to look for: a baby wrapped in a blanket and lying in a manger."

At once the angel was joined by a huge angelic choir singing God' praises:

Glory to God in the heavenly heights.

Peace to all men and women on earth who please him.

Thank You, God, for sending us the miracle of Your Son.

choose your destiny
464

ignite your spirit

choose your destiny

466

ignite your spirit

choose your destiny

ignite your spirit

choose your destiny

ignite your spirit

choose your destiny

ignite your spirit

list of scriptures in alphabetical order

Scripture	Date
1 Chronicles 4:10	2/2
1 Corinthians 8:6	3/21
1 John 1:7, 9	1/16
1 John 5:5,11-12	1/30
1 John 5:13	1/13
1 Peter 5:8	2/22
1 Thessalonians 4:13-14	4/3
1 Thessalonians 4:15-16	4/4
1 Thessalonians 4:17-18	4/5
1 Thessalonians 5:2	4/6
1 Thessalonians 5:3	1/23
1 Thessalonians 5:3	4/24
1 Thessalonians 5:16-18	10/5
1 Timothy 4:4-5	2/4
2 Corinthians 3:14-17	2/12
2 Corinthians 5:17,21	3/4
2 Corinthians 12:9	3/12
Acts 3:6-7	3/26
Acts 3:13,15-16	3/27
Acts 4:11-12	1/7
Acts 15:11	4/1
Colossians 3:1-2	2/3
Colossians 3:15	1/31
Colossians 3:16	3/23
Colossians 3:17	2/8
Daniel 2:20-21	3/8

Daniel 6:22	10/3
Deuteronomy 32:39	10/1
Ecclesiastes 3:1	9/9
Ecclesiastes 12:13	9/10
Ephesians 2:4-5	1/28
Ephesians 2:8-10	2/27
Ephesians 3:20-21	3/28
Ephesians 4:4-5-6	1/29
Ephesians 4:7,11-12	3/1
Ephesians 4:17-18	3/29
Ephesians 1:7-8	1/15
Galatians 2:16	3/17
Hebrews 6:19-20	3/5
Hebrews 1:1	12/11
Hebrews 1:2	12/12
Hebrews 1:3	12/13
Hebrews 1:4	12/14
Hebrews 1:5	12/15
Hebrews 1:6	12/16
Hebrews 1:7	12/17
Hebrews 1:8	12/18
Hebrews 1:9	12/19
Hebrews 1:12	12/22
Hebrews 1:13	12/23
Hebrews 1:14	12/24
Hebrews 1:10	12/20
Hebrews 1:11	12/21
Hebrews 11:1	3/7
Hebrews 12:12-14	3/6
Isaiah 55:8	1/24
Isaiah 43:1-2	4/11
Isaiah 43:3-4	4/12
Isaiah 43:5	4/13
Isaiah 43:6-7	4/14

Isaiah 55:6	2/18
James 2:1	2/16
James 5:13-14	1/8
Jeremiah 29:11	1/26
Jeremiah 29:13-14	1/27
Job 33:31-33	3/9
John 7:16-17	3/25
John 3:16	1/12
John 6:28-35	3/18
John 14:1	8/11
John 14:2	8/12
John 14:3	8/13
John 14:6	8/14
John 14:27	1/14
John 14:14-15,17	1/20
John 15:1,2, 4	2/9
Jude 1:24-25	4/2
Lamentations 3:22-24	2/29
Luke 2:6-7	12/25
Luke 2:8	12/26
Luke 2:9-10	12/27
Luke 2:11	12/28
Luke 2:12	12/29
Luke 2:13	12/30
Luke 6:38	3/11
Luke 10:37	1/19
Luke 14:13-14	10/4
Luke 17:14-15	2/25
Luke 18:16-17	3/20
Luke 2:14 &	
Luke 2:6-14	12/31
Matthew 6:33-34	10/2
Matthew 6:7-13	3/2
Matthew 7:1-2	2/15

Matthew 19:14	1/18
Philippians 3:7	3/3
Philippians 4:6-7	2/10
Philippians 4:12-13	2/19
Proverbs 1:7	1/10
Proverbs 3:1-2	1/11
Proverbs 3:5	8/2
Proverbs 3:6	8/3
Proverbs 3:12	8/4
Proverbs 3:15	8/5
Proverbs 3:21-23	8/6
Proverbs 4:1	8/7
Proverbs 4:6	8/8
Proverbs 4:26	8/15
Proverbs 9:12	4/15
Proverbs 10:1	11/10
Proverbs 10:2	11/11
Proverbs 10:3	11/12
Proverbs 10:4	11/13
Proverbs 10:5	11/14
Proverbs 10:6	11/15
Proverbs 10:7	11/16
Proverbs 10:8	11/17
Proverbs 10:9	11/18
Proverbs 10:10	11/19
Proverbs 10:11	11/20
Proverbs 10:12	11/21
Proverbs 10:13	11/22
Proverbs 10:14	11/23
Proverbs 10:15	11/24
Proverbs 10:16	11/25
Proverbs 10:17-18	11/26
Proverbs 10:19	11/27
Proverbs 10:20	11/28

Proverbs 10:21	11/29
Proverbs 10:22	11/30
Proverbs 10:23	12/1
Proverbs 10:24	12/2
Proverbs 10:25	12/3
Proverbs 10:26	12/4
Proverbs 10:27	12/5
Proverbs 10:28	12/6
Proverbs 10:29	12/7
Proverbs 10:30	12/8
Proverbs 10:31	12/9
Proverbs 10:32	12/10
Proverbs 12:4	4/16
Proverbs 12:5	4/17
Proverbs 12:6	4/18
Proverbs 12:7	4/19
Proverbs 17:22	1/9
Proverbs 27:1-2	2/13
Proverbs 27:5	3/15
Proverbs 28:13	2/5
Proverbs 29:18	2/11
Psalm 1:1	4/20
Psalm 1:2-3	4/21
Psalm 1:4-5	4/22
Psalm 1:6	4/23
Psalm 2:2-3	4/25
Psalm 2:11	4/26
Psalm 3:3-4	2/26
Psalm 4:1	4/27
Psalm 4:6-7	4/28
Psalm 4:8	4/29
Psalm 5:2-3	4/30
Psalm 6:2	4/7
Psalm 6:3	4/8

Psalm 6:4	5/1
Psalm 6:8-9	5/2
Psalm 7:1	5/3
Psalm 8:3-4	5/4
Psalm 8:5	5/5
Psalm 8:6-8	5/6
Psalm 8:9	5/7
Psalm 9:1	5/8
Psalm 9:2	5/9
Psalm 9:3	5/10
Psalm 9:4	5/11
Psalm 9:5	5/12
Psalm 9:6	5/13
Psalm 9:7-8	5/14
Psalm 9:8	5/15
Psalm 9:9	5/16
Psalm 9:10	5/17
Psalm 9:11	5/18
Psalm 9:12	5/19
Psalm 9:13	5/20
Psalm 9:14	5/21
Psalm 9:15	5/22
Psalm 9:16	5/23
Psalm 9:17	5/24
Psalm 9:18	5/25
Psalm 9:19	5/26
Psalm 9:20	5/27
Psalm 10:1	5/28
Psalm 10:2	5/29
Psalm 10:3	5/30
Psalm 10:4	5/31
Psalm 10:5	6/1
Psalm 10:6	6/2
Psalm 10:7	6/3

Psalm 10:8	6/4
Psalm 10:9	6/5
Psalm 10:10	6/6
Psalm 10:11	6/7
Psalm 10:12	6/8
Psalm 10:13	6/9
Psalm 10:14	6/10
Psalm 10:15	6/11
Psalm 10:16	6/12
Psalm 10:17	6/13
Psalm 10:18	6/14
Psalm 11:1	6/15
Psalm 11:2	6/16
Psalm 11:3	6/17
Psalm 11:4	6/18
Psalm 11:5	6/19
Psalm 11:6	6/20
Psalm 11:7	6/21
Psalm 12:1	6/22
Psalm 12:2	6/23
Psalm 12:3	6/24
Psalm 12:4	6/25
Psalm 12:5	6/26
Psalm 12:6	6/27
Psalm 12:7	6/28
Psalm 12:8	6/29
Psalm 13:1	6/30
Psalm 13:2	7/1
Psalm 13:3	7/2
Psalm 13:4	7/3
Psalm 13:5	7/4
Psalm 13:6	7/5
Psalm 14:1	7/6
Psalm 14:2	7/7

Psalm 14:3	7/8
Psalm 14:4	7/9
Psalm 14:5	7/10
Psalm 14:6	7/11
Psalm 14:7	7/12
Psalm 15:1	7/13
Psalm 15:2	7/14
Psalm 15:3	7/15
Psalm 15:4	7/16
Psalm 15:5	7/17
Psalm 16:1	7/18
Psalm 16:2	7/19
Psalm 16:3	7/20
Psalm 16:4	7/21
Psalm 16:5	7/22
Psalm 16:6	7/23
Psalm 16:7	7/24
Psalm 16:8	7/25
Psalm 16:9	7/26
Psalm 16:10	7/27
Psalm 16:11	7/28
Psalm 18:1	7/29
Psalm 18:2	7/30
Psalm 18:3	7/31
Psalm 18:4	8/1
Psalm 18:12	8/9
Psalm 18:13	8/10
Psalm 18:20	8/17
Psalm 18:21	8/18
Psalm 18:22	8/19
Psalm 18:23	8/20
Psalm 18:24	8/21
Psalm 18:25	8/22
Psalm 18:26	8/23

Psalm 18:27	8/24
Psalm 18:28	8/25
Psalm 18:29	8/26
Psalm 18:30	8/27
Psalm 18:31	8/28
Psalm 18:32	8/29
Psalm 18:33	8/30
Psalm 18:34	8/31
Psalm 18:35	9/1
Psalm 18:36	9/2
Psalm 18:37	9/3
Psalm 18:38	9/4
Psalm 18:39	9/5
Psalm 18:40	9/6
Psalm 18:41	9/7
Psalm 18:42	9/8
Psalm 18:45	9/11
Psalm 18:46	9/12
Psalm 18:47	9/13
Psalm 18:48	9/14
Psalm 18:49	9/15
Psalm 18:50	9/16
Psalm 19:1	9/17
Psalm 19:2	9/18
Psalm 19:3	9/19
Psalm 19:4	9/20
Psalm 19:5	9/21
Psalm 19:6	9/22
Psalm 19:7	9/23
Psalm 19:8	9/24
Psalm 19:9	9/25
Psalm 19:10	9/26
Psalm 19:11	9/27
Psalm 19:12	9/28
Psalm 19:13	9/29

Psalm 23:1	1/1
Psalm 23:2	1/2
Psalm 23:3	1/3
Psalm 23:4	1/4
Psalm 23:5	1/5
Psalm 23:6 & Psalm 23:1-6	1/6
Psalm 24:1	4/9
Psalm 25:4-5	4/10
Psalm 27:1	10/6
Psalm 27:2	10/7
Psalm 27:3	10/8
Psalm 27:4	10/9
Psalm 27:5	10/10
Psalm 27:6	10/11
Psalm 27:7	10/12
Psalm 27:8	10/13
Psalm 27:9	10/14
Psalm 27:10	10/15
Psalm 27:11	10/16
Psalm 27:12	10/17
Psalm 27:13	10/18
Psalm 27:14	10/19
Psalm 31:7	9/16
Psalm 31:23-24	3/10
Psalm 37:3-5	3/16
Psalm 37:22-23	2/28
Psalm 46:1	10/20
Psalm 46:2	10/21
Psalm 46:3	10/22
Psalm 46:4	10/23
Psalm 46:5	10/24
Psalm 46:6	10/25
Psalm 46:7	10/26

Psalm 46:8	10/27
Psalm 46:9	10/28
Psalm 46:10	10/29
Psalm 46:11	10/30
Psalm 57:1-2	2/7
Psalm 93:1	10/31
Psalm 93:2	11/1
Psalm 93:3	11/2
Psalm 93:4	11/3
Psalm 93:5	11/4
Psalm 96:1-2	2/6
Psalm 135:15-18	2/24
Psalm 136:1	2/21
Psalm 138:3	2/23
Psalm 138:8	3/24
Psalm 19:14	9/30
Psalm 100:1	11/5
Psalm 100:2	11/6
Psalm 100:3	11/7
Psalm 100:4	11/8
Psalm 100:5	11/9
Psalm 115:1	2/14
Psalm 116:1-2,5-6	2/20
Romans 3:22-24	2/1
Romans 5:1	2/17
Romans 5:12	3/22
Romans 6:5-6	3/30
Romans 6:7-8	3/31
Romans 8:5-6	3/13
Romans 8:28	1/17
Romans 8:35,37	3/14
Romans 8:38-39	1/21
Romans 10:10-11	1/25
Romans 12:2	1/22
Romans 12:14-21	3/19

references

Authors, websites, chapters, books, and songs referenced in Ignite Your Spirit by dates.

January 3	Website http://bible.christianity.com and *A Book of Great Price: The Most Valuable Book You Own* (by David Jeremiah).
January 8	How to make a prayer box.
January 12	Song: "No One Ever Cared for Me Like Jesus."
January 15	Website www.Godtube.org.
January 18	Website www.discoveryclub.org.
January 20	Added Bible reference John 3:16. Read any version
January 24	Website www.intouch.org.
January 30	Website www.billygraham.org.
February 5	Added Bible reference Psalm 103:12. Read any version
February 7	How to make a prayer box.
February 9	Website www.lifesgreatestquestion.com/way_home.
February 20	Story about a dog.
February 23	Website http://bible.christianity.com
February 24	How to accept Jesus as your Savior
February 26	Website www.tatepublishing.com.

February 27	Website www.insight.org.
February 28	*The Purpose Driven Life* Rick Warren's book
February 29	Song: "Great Is Thy Faithfulness"
March 2	*God's Psychiatry* Rev. Charles L. Allen.
March 3	Website http://bible.christianity.com and click on Bible in a Year.
March 6	Website www.pilates.com
March 14	Song: "We Are More Than Conquerors"
March 19	Added Bible reference Romans 12:15 and 18. Read any version
March 22	Website www.Godtube.org.
March 23	Song: "Singing, I Go"
March 24	*The Purpose Driven Life* Rick Warren.
March 30	Song "I Am the Resurrection" and *Added Bible reference John 11:25–26 (KJV).*
April 3	Website www.lifesgreatestquestion.com/way_home.html
April 5	Song: "Oh, That Will Be Glory"
April 14	*Israel in Crisis* David Dolan
April 19	Song: "Under His Wings"
April 23	Added reference Psalms 6:1–6 (TMB)
April 26	Song: "Joy to the World"
May 5	Website www.creationmuseum.com.
May 6	Song: "I Believe in Miracles"
May 12	Website http://bible.christianity.com
May 16	Song: "A Mighty Fortress Is Our God"

May 18	Song: "Praise Him! Praise Him!"
May 21	Song: "Awesome God"
May 24	Magnet "Heaven Is Real Do You Have Reservations?"
May 28	How to make a prayer box.
June 2	Website http://oneplace.com
June 7	Added Bible reference Romans 12:19 (NISV)
June 12	Song: "He's a Wonderful Saviour to Me"
June 14	Psalm 10:1–18 (TMB)
June 15	Website: http://bible.christianity.com
June 21	Psalm 11:1–7 (TMB)
June 26	Website www.focusonthefamily.com
June 29	Psalm 12:1–8 (TMB)
July 5	Psalm 13:1–6 (TMB) and song "Great Is Thy Faithfulness"
July 8	Randy Travis, Fox TV interview
July 12	Psalm 14:1–7 (TMB)
July 17	Psalm 15:1–5 (TMB)
July 28	Psalm 16:1–11 (TMB)
July 30	The song "The Solid Rock"
August 1	*Life after Death* Billy Graham
August 8	How to make a prayer box.
August 9	Song: "Jesus is Coming Again"
August 13	Song: "Solid Rock"
August 22	First half of chapter Psalm 18:1–25 from (TMB)

September 3	Song: "What a Friend We Have In Jesus"
September 6	Website www.lifesgreatestquestion.com/way-home.
September 10	*The Purpose Driven Life* Rick Warren
September 17	Website www.creationmuseum.com.
September 22	Song: "This Is My Father's World"
September 23	Website http://bible.christianity.com
September 30	Psalm 19:1–14 (TMB)
October 1	Song "God of Our Fathers"
October 5	How to make a prayer box.
October 19	Psalm 27:1–14 (TMB)
October 20	Psalm 23:1–6 (NISV)
October 21	Song "Tell it To Jesus"
October 23	Revelation 22:1 (KJV)
October 30	Psalm 46:1–11 (TMB)
November 3	Song: "A Mighty Fortress Is Our God"
November 4	Psalm 93:1–5 (TMB)
November 9	Psalm 100:1–5 (TMB)
November 15	Song: "There Shall Be Showers of Blessing"
November 21	How to make a prayer box.
December 3	Website www.Jesus2020.com.
December 6	Added Bible reference John 3:16 any version
December 10	Proverbs 10:1–32 (TMB)

December 12	Added Bible reference John 14: 6 any version
December 16	Song: "Holy Holy Holy!"
December 24	Hebrews 1:1–14 (TMB)
December 25	Added Bible verse Luke 2:11 (KJV)
December 30	Website www.Jesus2020.com
December 31	Luke 2:6–14 (TMB)